Caregiver

Caregiver

A Reluctant Extrovert

Susan Brown Hurst

ISBN 979-8-9863711-0-8
Caregiver A Reluctant Extrovert
Cover design by Susan Brown Hurst
Editing by Dayna Hurst Greskoff
Disclaimer: Medical information by the author is not meant to diagnose Myelofibrosis or any other MPN. Always consult a medical doctor for a correct diagnosis. The author does not have a medical degree.

Printed in the United States of America
First printing Edition

Author Contact Information
Website Susanbrownhurst.com
Facebook https://www.facebook.com/Susanbrownhurst
Twitter https://twitter.comSue
Email Sahurst61@gmail.com

Dedication Page

I authored this book for you, reader,
those who feel like a lifeguard that cannot swim.
Stay the course. You will find a new you!

Be ye strong therefore and let not your hands be weak:
for your work shall be rewarded.
2 Chronicles 15-7:

CONTENTS

PROLOGUE

The fact of the matter is that we are not going to make it out of this world alive. That seems like a sad first line, but I know that there is a promise that we will not endure physical or emotional struggles forever.

All of us will experience being a caregiver in one form or another. Sometimes we care for our children. Sometimes we care for our parents. But this is the story of my experience with caring for my partner, my best friend, and the love of my life: my husband.

Difficulties might seem to be consuming your life right now. It is a balance between watching, participating, and surviving. Days will be intertwined with joyous moments, closer relationships, and God's promise of grace.
And love.

Walk with me as I learned and earned experiences through Dan's journey and became a better caregiver, partner, wife, and better friend.

JOURNEY BEGINS

"Patience and fortitude conquer all things."

-Ralph Waldo Emerson-

Cast of Character

There are many Casts of characters in this book, but there would be no book without my husband, Dan. He is hard-working, loyal, and a bit of a work-out freak. His life was turned upside down by cancer. My husband's story became my story.

CHAPTER 1

ECEMBER 2015 BEGAN with my husband's health issues. He had a racing heart. His primary doctor sent him to a cardiologist, who did some routine tests, including the CBC or Complete Blood Count. The cardiologist was concerned about the results; she contacted our primary doctor. She also sent him to have an echocardiogram and more bloodwork, which resulted in an appointment with an oncologist, Dr. Rachel, in Mount Holly, New Jersey. It was a terrifying moment for both of us. What was going on?

The oncologist ordered a full panel blood test. The results suggested a Bone Marrow Biopsy would be needed to determine what type of cancer Dan had.

My first actual baby-step caregiver moment was the bone biopsy experience. The oncologist offered to do the biopsy in the office. After hearing the procedure, Dan opted to be sedated, which involved him going into the hospital as an out-patient, having light anesthesia, recovery then home.

Why does everything have to happen at dawn? We arrived by 6 a.m. to have his vitals and paperwork completed, and then the wait. The doctor, anesthetist, and nurse shared information about the procedure and asked Dan to sign the forms.

*Interjection:

Is it just me who thinks there must be a better way for hospital staff to share crucial last-minute information before surgery? Do you have a Living Will? Do you want us to resuscitate you?" Seriously? You might need to do that now! *

He was given an epidural and numbed in the hip area where the extraction would occur. Using an MRI scan, the doctor targeted the area and began inserting a needle, which Dan said must have been square, and removing a bit of tissue and fluid. Dan said, "It was very unnerving feeling pain in your inside." It was over in about 30 minutes, while the recovery room took 3 hours. Being by his side and helping him through this was scary for me, and I must admit, I was ill-prepared. I caught a bit of anxiety and turned part of the day about me. (More about me and elevators later). He was in discomfort for several days but did not miss a day of work in true Dan fashion.

Waiting three weeks for the biopsy results to come back was tough. I was trying to figure out how to set my feelings aside and show support to Dan. I did not want him to see me upset, which would make him upset. I decided to always be his cheerleader and never let him down. Impossible to accomplish, but a goal, nonetheless. I had a lot to learn.

In November of 2016, the diagnosis was Primary Myelofibrosis. Dr. Rachel had explained the cancer was slow-growing and did not have stages like other cancers but had phases. His was in the beginning phase. I thought, "great"; it is not something that will take him away." Time is a funny thing.

"Time and tide wait for no man." Geoffrey Chaucer

Technical Stuff

Myelofibrosis is a rare bone marrow cancer that causes fibrosis (scarring) in the bone marrow to build up, causing the cells to form incorrectly and be sent out to the bloodstream too early. That means infection-fighting cells (white) and oxygen (red), over time, will stop producing healthy cells to keep his body functioning.

I jumped in with both feet doing online research and learning what each blood test meant. God indeed created a unique, complex body. Tiny, little things like cells run around and do an excellent job unless they do not. How did he get this awful condition, and how could it be fixed? He has a somatic mutation in the Janus Kinase 2 (JAK2) gene. Although some research suggests it can pass to your children, his parents did not have the mutated gene. Most patients have no symptoms and find out during routine blood work, generally in their 50s. Two other blood disorders are in his cancer group, Myeloproliferative Neoplasms (known commonly as MPNs): Essential Thrombocythemia (ET) and Polycythemia Vera (PV). All are characterized by increased proliferation of myeloid, megakaryocytic, and erythroid cells. Very few in the Oncology world agreed on treatment.

Research has an ugly side: it is a terrific way to become more concerned and confused. The bottom line was that he had five years to live unless he opted for a Stem Cell Transplant, which the doctor did not recommend at this phase.

After my research, I called crying to my parents; would I grow old with my husband? The profound sadness I felt is not describable. I did not know how to help him or me. At work, I shared the information with a co-worker and friend, Rachael. She became one of my strongest supporters. Dan knew I was sad. When married for 32 years, it is easy to tell each other's feelings without words.

I am the positive person, and he the negative, or as he likes to say, a realist. Our faith has always been strong, and we never wavered in knowing the Lord was there; For me, I just faltered with how I was to listen. This would be the most significant growth, listening.

Wait

In our infinite human wisdom, Dan and I thought that he was the healthiest he would be at that moment and should have the Stem Cell Transplant (SCT). Dr. Rachel, our oncologist, wanted us to use the "wait and see" method, meaning it was slow-growing, do not mess with it. This did not sit well with Dan or me. We are active doers. But we went with her suggestion and worked on his diet.

We looked at holistic treatments through infusions, but Dan was not willing at $2,000 a month, but I was! Our daughter-in-love Elise is excellent in nutrition and helped us with a food plan. (She later received her Master's in Nutrition). He could follow most of her suggestions but, like any plan, had to change some things. I made him a shake of kefir, banana, raw honey, turmeric, and cinnamon every day, except on weekends. He would take a shake to work and drink it during the day. It was not optimum timing, but it worked to stabilize his energy/sugar level.

Dan was 58 when he was diagnosed. He has lifted weights since he was 14. He also is a 4th-degree blackbelt. At his age, he was doing 100 sit-ups, 70+ pushups, and lifting weights every day except Sunday. He has always maintained a healthy weight, and although he was not the best of eaters, he managed to keep his high school weight. I will not tell you how far I am from my high school weight, but I can live on a deserted island for weeks without food!

Our favorite vacation was on a cruise ship. He would run around the boat and work out in the gym as often as possible while I relaxed by the pool and read a book. (Excellent example of why I did not maintain my high school weight). Sometimes I would read a book IN the pool. We were each doing what we loved, separate but together. We were content!

When To Tell Others

We decided it was time to tell others about Dan's cancer. It was obvious he was becoming more fatigued and his legs, tired. Of course, the immediate family knew initially, but our employers and friends were another matter. Dan did not want anyone to treat him differently, including folks' sympathetic looks.

I had a very dear friend, Ana, diagnosed with stage 4 lung cancer, while Dan was diagnosed with Myelofibrosis. We often talked about her feelings about others' treatment and how Dan dealt with the same. Neither wanted that "look." She described it as the sad look, the "oh, you're going to die" look. After a while, it just unnerved her. But she also said she got it; it is not easy to know what to say or do. Both Ana and Dan wanted, needed, to feel normal. I did not get this at first. I wanted him to stop doing his workouts, retire from work, and chill. I want to say I supported him, but I did not. I was supporting myself. I tried to put him in a bubble. Ana helped me to see the harm it would cause. She was a fantastic friend.

We started by telling our places of work. The news began trickling out little by little that Dan was sick. Dan turned it into something he could manage by turning it into a joke. He had some fun playing the "C" card with his friends. That made it bearable. As the months and years went by, the less family and friends seemed to talk about it. So many people have their struggles. I lost an uncle, aunt, cousin, and Dan's friends lost family members. Suffering does not pass by anyone. But in our reality, in our bubble, sometimes it is hard to see others, or we do not have the strength to bear more.

Photographed by Dan in Yellowstone National Park in July 2021

9

FEEL NORMAL

Normal: conforming to a type, standard, or regular pattern: characterized by that which is considered usual, typical, or routine normal.

-Merriam-Webster Dictionary-

CHAPTER 2

I N 2017 AND 2018, we continued to plan our winter Florida vacations and our Pocono vacations every spring to keep the normalcy alive. We always felt the weight of his diagnosis, but there were times that it lessened enough to feel normal. We continued to see his oncologist in NJ every three months. In 2018, the fibrosis in his marrow was causing significant concerns. White blood cells (WBC) were rising alarmingly, and red blood cells (RBC) were getting "pushed" out of the crowded marrow not wholly formed.

We connected with a Stem Cell Transplant Team at the Abramson Cancer Center in Philadelphia (Penn) to understand what that would entail. Our oncologist in Mount Holly was associated with Penn.

In the spring of 2018, his oncologist said Dan should begin preparing for an SCT by September. We were surprised how quickly his blood numbers went in the wrong direction. His WBC count went into the high 90,000 range (normal is 4,500-11,000), and he also had anemia-related concerns. I asked others on an MPN site if they knew of anything that would hold off or even cure Myelofibrosis and landed on Interferon or PEGASYS injections. All in God's timing. Our oncologist in NJ was on board, but we had to go through the Abramson Cancer Center at The University of Penn since it was a specialty medication. Back to the SCT Team, where we met Dr. James.

Finding the Right Doctor

I want to pause a moment here. I cannot strongly tell you how vital patient and doctor cohesiveness is. We have seen some doctors who made us wonder why they even showed up to work or others that just seemed confused. We were blessed to find an oncologist in NJ and even doctors at Penn who collaborated well with us. Dan is a funny guy and sometimes complex. He has an extensive vocabulary and is a people person. He likes his doctors to be down-to-earth and confident. He relies on their experience and expertise. He does what the doctors tell him to do. He will not second guess them once he has built the rapport. Second-guessing was my job) My husband is also a bit of a drama king. He tends to exaggerate concerns. If his shoulder hurts, he walks and moves like it is falling off! Hahaha. Stomach pain, which is gas, makes mouth noises like he will not be able to get up out of the chair! Overly dramatic. I say this not to pick on him but to encourage you to figure out your loved one and find a doctor who fits those needs. An easy-going, intellectual, down-to-earth, enthusiastic doctor with a sense of humor was what we needed and found!

Holistic vs. Conventional Medicine

We talked to the doctor at Penn about the information I read on the MPN support sites. Dr. James was in favor of us trying holistic methods. He explained that no studies suggest herbs, vitamins, and healthy foods would change the outcome overall but make his body stronger for a transplant. Eating foods from the earth was the best: vegetables, meats, and fruit. He was already eating healthy for the most part. The doctor spoke to his colleagues, and they agreed interferon was known to help manage the white cell growth. PEGASYS (peginterferon alfa-2a) is an alpha-interferon, which had been around for years, but has not been studied for myelofibrosis, but those using it on the MPN site showed satisfactory results. This was a God moment: perfect timing. So began in the spring of 2018 with the weekly self-injections and two-week visits.

Dan used to faint at the sight of needles; now, he was injecting himself. Some of the side effects were hard to deal with: foggy brain, achiness, and sometimes a low-grade fever. Through it all, he managed to work and work out. He would go for bloodwork every two weeks to check that his RBC count was not getting too low, one of the side effects. We did not see much change in his bloodwork for the first three months. Others on the MPN site told us to hang in there and wait. Then boom, just like that, the blood numbers turned around at three months. When we went to the doctors at Penn and were told he was doing so well, we only needed to see the doctor every three months again, and self-injections changed to every two weeks.

We cried in the underground parking garage at Penn. The WBC count came down; the RBC count was steady. It is working! We knew God was sustaining him! We knew God led me to that MPN site to give us more time. Healing is not forever; healing is God's grace for time. Complete healing is when we see Him! We felt blessed!

DAN AND HIS SONS

"Of all the titles I have been privileged to have 'Dad' has always been the best".

-Ken Norton-

CHAPTER 3

THERE ARE VERY few things in which Dan takes pride. He is not a prideful person, except with his sons. We have three amazing sons. I know I sound like a mom, but it is true. Eric, Tim, and Nicholas, respectively. They are our hearts. Each brings into our life different adventures. Each took Dan's condition differently. At diagnosis, our oldest, Eric, was 30, Tim 26, and Nicholas 25. Dan is remarkably close to his boys. Before diagnosis, Dan planned to take each son on a separate father-son vacation. A memorable trip to bond. Nicholas was the first to take his journey before Dan's diagnosis. They went to Europe for nine days. They created a trip, rented a car, and explored France, Switzerland, Belgium, and a smattering of Germany. They both love history, had an exciting time, lots of laughs, got lost in a storm, and, well, that is a story for a different time.

After Dan's appointment in January 2018, I spoke to Tim and encouraged him to pursue his father-son trip while Dan was feeling okay. Erin, his wife, also pushed Tim to go. Her mom had cancer and passed later that year, in May of 2018. Even though Erin was enduring so much pain for her mom, she encouraged Tim not to miss a second with his dad. Amazing woman!

Dan and Tim picked Yellowstone National Park for June 2018. Dan's hemoglobin was at 8 (most likely from his weekly injections), but Dr. James at Penn okayed the trip and gave him two units of blood to bring his hemoglobin up to 10.4 about two weeks before they left. Dan felt wonderful. Hiking, quads, hot springs, and camping in an open field during a summer storm (storms during father-son trips seem to be the norm) were just a few memories. We do not have funds to speak of, but Dan's mother and I made sure they got the best of everything. Through months of calling every day, I got a room in Old Faithful Lodge, the oldest section of the hotel. Dan had gone there years ago and always wanted to stay in the old section. I flew them first-class, as a surprise, although two flights were in small planes (which just meant they had more leg room!), they appreciated it.

Eric's father-son trip is planned for Alaska. We are not sure when that will occur, but they look forward to their time together. Both wanted to wait until after he was better: something to look forward to.

Stable

After the Yellowstone trip, his condition was stable. He was able to continue working. The PEGASYS was working well, and he was symptom-free for one and a half years. We had many people praying for him. I call them our prayer warriors. Dan met a man on a cruise ship who prayed for him! He was so happy. I am grateful for the time of God's healing power for Dan physically and mentally.

2018 quickly turned into 2019. In October of 2019, his WBC began to climb again. It rose to 78,000. (Again, normal is between 4,500 and 11,000.) The Interferon was not keeping the fibrosis at bay. Dan's specialist, Dr. James from Penn, moved to California to take another position in August 2019. We saw his new oncologist at Penn once in September 2019 before she left on a six-month sabbatical with a scheduled return in March

2020. Dr. Elizabeth, Dan's new doctor, tweaked his medication before she went, and his WBC and RBC leveled again. We thought about finding another doctor but stayed with the University of Penn since we liked the nurse practitioner and felt that going elsewhere was not in his best interest. The new doctor taught our past doctor about MPNs; he would be in good hands.

I must mention our amazing jobs. Dan worked for L&L Redi Mix. He had been there for 33 years. I worked for an Assistant Living Facility for ten years. Both companies were so flexible, allowing us to go into work late or have whatever time we needed to take Dan to expected or unexpected appointments. Having a sickness over your head is hard enough, but both employers gave us help and support. We will forever be thankful for that and other things they have done.

In December 2019, Dan had a blood transfusion to help with his lowering RBC. Although the newly adjusted medications helped, it was like a bandage that would not hold the wound much longer. Dan went through a time of sadness, and, as always, his family and friends surrounded him with love and humor. How much longer would his body sustain him? I was still focusing on food, appointments, and keeping his spirits up. Caregiving is a mixture of emotional and physical tasks to make life work. I am a "fixer." I learned a hard lesson; I cannot fix everything and should not.

Dan's 67 Chevy, Eric, Nicholas, and Tim

Top: Nicholas, Eric, Dan, Sue, Erin, Tim
Bottom: Rachel, Elise, Bryce Brendon, Hayleigh, Alyson, Aubrey
(Nolan was born the following year)
Photographs by Rebecca Sittig (niece) 08/2020

CORONAVIRUS DISEASE COVID-19

"The world has changed and it's going to keep changing, but God never changes; so we are safe when we cling to Him."

-Charles R. Swindoll-

CHAPTER 4

COVID-19 WAS PRESENTED in January 2020. Many things changed for all of us, but the change was profound for those working or staying in hospitals. I worked in an assisted living facility and was concerned I could bring home COVID-19 to Dan. It could be fatal if he were to get SARS in his immune-compromised state. This was a caregiver moment I struggled with. Many at my work were concerned about bringing it home to loved ones. We all couldn't stop working. I spoke with Rachael again (supervisor) and reached out to Jen, my director. I left on Family Medical Leave for four weeks to see how my facility would cope with their protocols. They did very well, so I returned knowing the protocols and balance were in place. I did not like leaving my co-workers during that rough period, but I had to put Dan first in the end.

*Interjection:

While others stayed home, my co-workers and their staff worked and covered for those of us who couldn't. I wish I could name them all. I pray God blessed them. *

Masks, masks, masks…I am not a fan of masks! They serve a purpose, but, boy, are they irritating. I refused to purchase cute ones, but I have been given a few as gifts. Masks and cleaning became the norm at home and work. Visiting my parents in their 80s, or anyone seeing us, had to comply with our protocols. The plant he worked at had a few folks who, if they got COVID-19, would be at high risk, so they were all cautious. Dan stayed in his truck and would not let anyone else use it. I would wipe down any areas someone else had been in at work—what a crazy life and an extra caregiving concern.

Additional Heartache

In April 2020, it became apparent that my father needed a new valve in his heart. The "leaking" valve made his heart work harder and enlarge. When he walked, he felt out of breath. He also had kidney problems and breathing concerns. After downsizing, my mother, 86, and my father, 85, lived in a mobile home. Dad was a truck driver working at the same place Dan worked until retiring at age 72. Mom had a stroke a few years back, her eyesight being the most affected. Dad did all the driving, shopping, and, well, seeing. They had five children: Bill (wife Eileen) in New Jersey, Kathy in Texas, Ernie (wife Barb, who I fondly called Auntie Mable) in Iowa, and Me (Sue, Susie, or Susan) and Rick (wife Nikki) in Pennsylvania. All were doing what they could to help ease my parents. While Dad was getting weaker, I tried being there for them both, but I was back to work and coping with the ever-growing concern that Dan was coming close to having to make a hard decision.

Transfusion Dependent and Life Decision

Dan needed a unit of blood in December, March, and June; he had become transfusion dependent. Without the transfu-sions, he would not be able to function. The oncologist said it was time to talk about the transplant. This time Dan was ready and even eager. He had had enough. He was tired of this being over his head every day and was ready to smack it around on his terms.

On June 4th, 2020, Dan and I had a telehealth video chat with his oncologist, Dr. Elizabeth, Dan's new doctor. (Telehealth calls were because of COVID-19, but we liked them; it was much easier than heading to Philly.) Dan's condition was quickly moving into Acute Myeloid Leukemia, or AML, which meant that the window for a successful transplant was closing. Once closed, it could not be opened without being behind the 8-ball. He asked if he did not get a transplant, would he be alive in five years? No. Two? No. Once he had AML, she said he would have about a year. I stayed out of the decision-making except to ask questions to help Dan see the choices. It was important to me that he makes the choice. He needed to be strongly committed to going through the fight for his life. And he was! He was ready. "Let's do it now!" So, the plan was set. There is a lot to do to get all the ducks in a row for a Stem Cell Transplant, including insurance, medical, and financial. Waiting was hard for him. He was ready now! All in God's timing.

I did not realize it then; life would get tough. Life as I knew it was going to change. There are guaranteed truths that, although I knew would happen, I always thought, "Someday — it will happen someday. Not now, not today." The following year would test endurance, strength, and faith. My partner — my love — needed me, and I would be there, no matter what.

Donor

In 2019 our children and his sister were tested; all were five out of 10 matches. Although a familiar match of five is good, the best is a donor that is a 10 out of 10 match. Dr. Elizabeth said they had several 10/10 matches in the donor pool. Dan was pleased that the family members were not complete matches since if he did not make it, he did not want that weighing on whoever was chosen. His donor was a 20-year-old female, apparently from Germany. Such a wonderful gift. She had the cells extracted, frozen, and sent by courier plane. Years ago, this was not possible, but through the marvel of science, a frozen specimen was able to be thawed and used. We asked if it would hurt her, but it is a simple blood removal like giving blood at a blood bank, except they take the blood and break it down to extract the cells. Amazing!

FAMILY

"Promise me you'll always remember that you are braver than you believe, stronger than you seem, and smarter than you think".

Christopher Robin to Winnie the Pooh
-A.A. Milne-

CHAPTER 5

ROUND THIS SAME time, it was apparent that my father-in-law Bill, 86, suffered from Alzheimer's. He loved to shop, taking his scooter with coupons in tow to different stores for that amazing bargain. Walking was his exercise program with an average of eight miles a day. Neighbors often saw him walking, crisscrossing down the street to get his steps. My 85-year-old mother-in-law, Barbara, is healthy. She beat Polio as a seven-year-old child and rose in the banking industry as one of the first women to jump into the "Men's Club." Both are strong, wonderful people. My in-laws, Bill and Barbara, paid for Dan's initial tests to take the burden off us. Bill worked for Boeing Vertol for years and retired with travel and shopping in mind. Now both our fathers were dealing with life changes, and in turn, so were our mothers—so many curveballs. Dan has a brother Dave (wife Nancy) in Alaska, a sister Dayna (husband Michael) in Pennsylvania, and a smattering of cousins, nieces, and nephews. Dayna's son Jake helps Barbara with caregiving Bill. Dan's family has been an enormous reason Dan is doing so well. He has a great support system, even from those located far away.

Healthy Otherwise

Our family and his doctors often said that "he is healthy, otherwise." I clung to that phrase as my mantra. When folks asked me how he was doing, I always said that mantra. I did not know what else to say. My husband was slowly losing the battle. His body was giving up. He had to give up "side jobs" of concrete work and karate. His mom and I bought him an electric bike to go on vacation and be mobile since his legs were so tired. His bones ached. He came to the fork in the road and chose the option of a chance at life. He was tired of being in his own body, the body that began to fight him at every corner. COVID-19 limited the sphere of friends and family he could be around. The hardest part of COVID-19 was not seeing loved ones, especially his father. Would he recognize Dan?

Not too Late

In August, we had a face-to-face with Dr. Elizabeth. She laid out the pros and cons again. "Not too late to change your mind," "long road," "at least a year to recover," "strong medications," and a "committed caregiver or three" were all parts of the conversation. She wanted to make sure he understood. He seemed "more eager than most." He asked a few additional questions (really, I think he came up with a few to make his doctor feel better), but the one answer he heard was that eventually, his bones would be painful, and he would be unable to walk, even unable to get out of bed. It would leave him breathless, not able to work out. You get the picture.

It would be a prolonged and painful death. She talked about other options, but they were all band-aids, and again, once the window was closed and he had AML, there was lit-tle hope. He told her again that he was ready. It was in God's hands. And he meant it. Once he decided to give it entirely over to God, he never looked back.

GREEN FLAG RACING

"It is amazing how many drivers, even at the Formula One level, think that the brakes are for slowing the car down."

-Mario Andretti-

CHAPTER 6

IT WAS TIME to get everything in order; prepare the house, his Will, finances, caregivers, schedules, food lists, stock products, etc. There was an enormous amount to do to give him the best chance. I was not going to leave one stone unturned. We spent about $2,000 getting rid of old rugs and furniture and purchasing air purifiers and new furniture. Our sons got the heavy stuff out of the house while the daughters-in-love helped with the inside organizing and food. We set up a room for me to sleep in while he had a "suite" in our room. Even though I kept my circle small, there was always a chance I could carry something to him. Masks were our thing even before they were required for COVID-19. The first one hundred days post-SCT is the most dangerous for infections.

We refinanced the mortgage we shared with our son Nicholas to a lower rate and paid off all debts. We contacted Social Security and set up disability after Family Leave funds ran out. We completed his medical directives and his Will and asked our friends Mark and Sue to witness.

One of the most challenging emotional preps we did was a family meeting with our sons and daughters-in-love. We went over schedules, where I needed help, what to do if I became sick, Dan's Will, and essential papers. This must have been hard for Erin, who had recently lost her mom to cancer. She was her mom's primary caregiver and knew this would be hard. She had great insight. "A supporting friend is essential—someone who will listen," she said. I immediately thought of my long-time friend Deborah. Our supportive families were always there, but they were helping mom and dad.

Erin is an incredible coordinator. When she sees a problem, she finds a way to fix it and make it better than before. She was my go-to gal for any catering or social activities. She knew how important this last step for Dan and me needed to be set.

Everyone added their thoughts and concerns. My family loves to laugh, and the laughter added in was helpful. After two hours, they understood the plan that Dan and I made and what to expect for the most part. They would jump in where they could, but reality has a check for kids, work, and life. I would be the primary caregiver after he came home. During our marriage ceremony, I committed to sickness or in health. I will always honor my husband. Two other hospital caregivers would be his sister, Dayna, and mom.

We thought Dan would start his SCT in late August, but insurance had a few hoops for us to jump through to get the okay. Dealing with insurance was extremely easy. We had a Life Source Coordinator from Cigna, Melissa, who walked us through it and was a great help. She was genuinely kind, and since Penn was a Life Source Hospital with our Insurance company, it was just a matter of getting the required tests done and final approval. His heart, by the way, was fine. The racing was too many caffeinated beverages.

My time was spent setting up the house to make it safe and prepping for appointments and paperwork.

*Interjection:

I have spoken to other caregivers who have struggled with medical insurance quagmires, especially a veteran. I advise finding a health insurance broker who can be your go-between.

Connect with the financial department your doctor will use for billing…get a contact name. Set up Social Security Disability six months in advance. Pile of patience…start early! *

My brother Bill and wife Eileen offered us their house down the shore for an extended weekend. It was great to be away from the prep for a few days and enjoy the beautiful weather. His neighbor gave us a ride in the bay on his boat. We enjoyed a bit of kayaking and dealt with nasty little greenhead flies. You know about the flies if you have ever visited the Jersey shore!

Before SCT, part of the requirements was a class covering essential information and many do's and don'ts. On Bluejeans (Penn's version of Zoom), a nutritionist, nurse practitioner, and financial adviser shared valuable information. Dan had an Allogeneic (unrelated donor), while others had families donating cells. As we listened to the other patients asking questions and sharing their conditions, we were sad that many were sicker than Dan. Chemo was going to be more aggressive for them. I prayed for them, and inside I was very thankful it was not the same for Dan. But God knew we did not know what we were facing, and I am grateful we did not. Sometimes too much information leads to worry and stress.

Before his hospitalization, my last extensive prep (which took three days!) was a flurry of baking (health bars) and cooking to ensure that he had homemade snacks and meals for his hospital stay. Foods he could not eat included anything with fungi (bacteria concerns), citrus (medication interactions), soft cheese or blue cheese (mold concerns), acidic foods (stomach upset), some herbs, and red meat unless cooked to 165 degrees. Increased foods he needed:"good fats," pasta, dried fruits, some vegetables, and white meats (except for deli) and broths.

Looking back, it feels like I was trying to keep busy and distracted. It was a familiar coping mechanism. He could not eat most of the foods I prepared during his stay because of stomach issues, but I was able to contribute home comfort foods when he wanted. If I had to do it all over again, I would not have added the extra stress—learning moment.

Tip: Ask the food service staff to bring you a boxed guest meal. It saved on the expenses and my home meal prep for myself. I found the staff to be very accommodating.

My Father

In July, my father had open-heart surgery. His options were having it done or remaining a ticking time bomb. Wonderful choice. My dad does not do well in the hospital; he can be combative with the nurse's suggestions (put your feet up, walk, drink). My mom has always been able to encourage him. But COVID-19 happened. For the first two weeks, he was alone in the hospital. The nurses were excellent, but they were not my mom. He even knew one of the nurses, Carol, but it was not my mom again. By the end of July, they allowed visitors so she could visit for one half-hour every day.

I understand why COVID-19 was a scary scenario, but I think the toll it took on those left in the hospital for other issues far outweighed the concerns of a lockdown. He suffered greatly. He went to rehab and then back to the hospital with an infection. He came home again, then back in the hospital with another concern. We will never know what COVID-19 did to folks, but I know it hurt him not having mom there. He was having bouts of hallucinations but always knew my mom. Selfish as it may sound, that reality is mine.

During one of the times my father was home, Dan visited him to tell my dad how proud he was of him and hoped he would be as strong. Dan left, and my father cried. That was the last time they saw each other. We are thankful for that moment when father and "son" understood what they meant to one another. Both asked about each other often.

Bill and Arlene Brown: My Parents
(Photographed by Rebecca Sittig 2019)

Bill and Barbara Hurst
Dan's Parents

ALLOGENEIC (UNRELATED DONOR) STEM CELL TRANSPLANT FIGHT FOR THE CURE

"It's easier to take than to give. It's nobler to give than to take. The thrill of taking lasts a day. The thrill of giving lasts a lifetime."

-Joan Marques-

CHAPTER 7

WE HAD A date for SCT by the end of August, September 18th. The finishing touches were put into place, and we were as ready as possible. I spent the last night with my husband, not knowing when, or if, we would be Danny and Susie again. The University of Penn (HUP) hospital was to be his (and, in a way, my) home for a while. It was a 40-minute drive from door-to-door. Our son Eric took us on the first day and was a great support. He went back with Dan to have his PICC line placed. I was glad Eric was there; neither of us expected it to go into a vein near his heart. It made sense; I had just never thought of it. COVID-19 restrictions allowed only one person to go to the hospital room, but our son also managed to go. Dan shared a room for a day, then moved to a private room in the front of Rhodes Tower, Floor 7. He started chemo on the second day, three days of chemo, two days of rest, and one day of radiation. I was sad when the first chemo drug was going into his line. I cannot explain what it was but sadness. This beautiful, courageous man was having his life cells destroyed. Would the donor cells work? I prayed!

He had very few side effects in the first five days. His hair remained intact, no nausea, and he still had his appetite. The biggest problem was that he was lethargic. No matter how hard he tried to stay awake, he could not. At that time, he could drink caffeinated beverages, which helped, but there was not a lot I could do but sit with him. Hopefully, he felt my love.

Monday, September 21st, was our 35th wedding anniversary. Our son Nicholas and his girlfriend Rachel bought us a delicious tiny cake from Randolph Bakery in Marlton, New Jersey. We had permission from the SCT Team to have it because it was dairy. Usually, the Poconos was our anniversary destination each September, so we had gone in August to anticipate his hospitalization. Every fifth anniversary we exchanged new rings and went to unique places, like Nantucket, cruises, and Europe. Dan worked in an industry that destroyed rings, so we decided every five years to exchange rings. We did not exchange rings this time. Although it was his cure, I would not count on the hospital being special. We planned to exchange rings at a more festive time.

My Sweet Friend Ana

I mentioned Ana earlier. I have known Ana since we were in our early twenties. I met her through the church, along with her now-husband Tim. Through God's calling, Dan and I started a home school group called Living Water Home Educators in 1994. Tim and Ana joined and quickly became our sidekicks in leadership for 17 years. They had eight children; we raised three boys. Together we worked with over 90 families and 500 kids. She was my friend, my mentor, and my vent-listener. When she was 56, Ana was diagnosed with stage 4 lung cancer. We often chatted about her and Dan's condition and shared research. All her children love the Lord and genuinely are called according to His purpose; there are many stories I could share, but it is not my story to tell. I hope one day one of her amazing children will write a book about this generous and amazing women.

On September 21st, at the age of 58, her children and her husband sang her into the loving arms of Jesus.

I was asked to speak at Ana's funeral by her children. What an incredible, humbling feeling to be a part of her service. Our son Tim stayed with Dan in the hospital while I celebrated our sweet friend. Ana's family did a live stream, so others who could not be there could "attend." Dan and Tim were able to watch. After the service, I broke down in the pew and sat there for a while. A dear friend, Sherril, sat with me as I let my emotions spill over. She had lost her husband to cancer. There was just so much going on. How does anyone do this life without the Lord? Only He gave me enough peace and grace to put one foot in front of the other.

Hospital Restrictions

In the NJ hospital where my dad was, visitation increased to 30 minutes, then to two hours to visit patients. In PA, I was able to be there from 6 a.m. to 10 p.m. The hospitals in PA extended the visitor hours in the summer, which was perfect for Dan and me. They wanted the same person to visit each day, but it was more important to have others there when I could not be. I spoke to the head floor nurse when we originally toured, and she said they would allow more than just me, but she advised me to "keep the circle small." The schedule from our home meeting worked very well. I would visit Dan for three days, then go to work Thursday through Sunday since the other caregivers could be there on the weekends. Dan's sister Dayna went every Thursday, one of our sons Friday and Saturday, and his mom on Sunday.

Back to Me

I shared that the first BMB ended up being about me. I hate elevators. No, I step into one and almost pass out! For the past two years, when we went to Penn, Dan would drop me off at the front of the Perelman Center (connected with Abramson Cancer Center), and I would meet him on the 1st floor after he parked in the underground garage, and either walk up to the 4th floor or take the dreaded elevator. I missed out on visiting others in the hospital because I had to take an elevator. (My father was the exception.) This would be a significant part of this story if I relayed every clever way I avoided elevators. I was highly creative. But my knees are a problem. One is bone on bone; the other has a tear in the tendon that catches under my knee cap. My years of walking up steps without surgery are quickly ending. But it was funny because I had prayed about my fear of elevators for years, and now I had no choice but to "step on." God did answer my prayer, as always. As Dan's caregiver, I could categorize his needs over my fear. I still do not like elevators and will most likely not volunteer to ride one, but I am no longer afraid. At least the ones at Penn with Dan allowed me to see how slight my fear was in comparison. This was a huge victory. God gives us victories during times of trouble. This was one of many.

Dan was moved to a "waiting room" while they cleaned his room from top to bottom with bleach to prepare for the special donor cells. This was a critical moment. His room became an Allogeneic Stem Cell Transplant room. All who entered wore gowns, masks, and gloves. I also asked all the caregivers to change their shoes at the door and shower before coming. According to the class, many had animals, and the dander was a concern. When released from the hospital, those in the class who had animals at home had to have them bathed twice a week. The first 100 days, we kept hearing, were critical.

This was a rough day for him. He had a fever, felt achy, and was not mentally with it. After six hours, they moved him back to his room. He slept most of the time. It was so hard to know I would not be with him for the next four days. The nurses said he would feel better the next day. I'm glad I was there. Apparently, it was from the radiation used to kill whatever the chemo did not.

CAREGIVER LOGBOOK

logbook: "A logbook is a book in which someone records details and events relating to something, for example, a journey or period of their life."

-Merriam-Webster Dictionary-

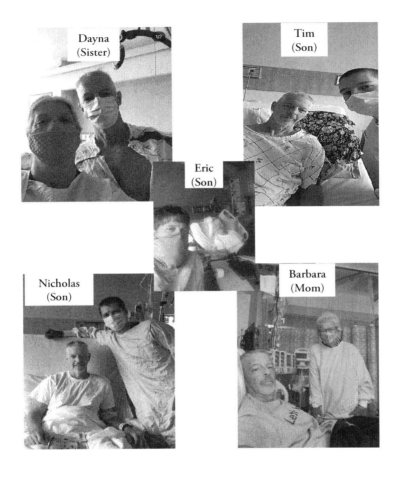

*Interjection:

Tim is remarkably like his father. He loves to work out and never complains. Like Eric, he has many family obligations, including three children, and does well. Tim wanted to be the one when it was time to find a donor. Our boys, Eric, Tim, and Nicholas ,were half matches, which was great in some cases. Tim was devastated when the doctors went with a 10/10 match and an outside donor. He shared with his brothers he wanted to be the one to donate. When Dan received his new cells, Tim was there. They were not his cells, but he was watching the cure. *

Saturday, September 26th Caregiver Eric (son)

"Dad took a shower around 10:45. He wanted me to add that he didn't walk yesterday but did so this morning. Dad struggled with energy during his shower. He is also experiencing hand tremors.

Activities during the day:

Teeth Brushed, Saltwater rinse, nose spray- 11:15 am

Dad's BP 129/78 11:35

Ate lunch 12:30pm

Saltwater rinse/teeth brushed-2:30pm

Dad told me he would start new meds tonight.

Walked 4 laps at 4:30 pm

Nose spray

Dads BP 123/67

Dad had diarrhea last night and 3 more bouts today.

The new medication is methotrexate (which suppresses his

immune system so the new donor cells will graft) on days +1, +3, +6, and +11 through his PICC line

*Interjection:

Eric is the first-born son. He and Dan share a love of language and spiritual theology. They both love to learn and research. The difference between Dan and Eric is Eric loves to speak in public. He is funny, intellectual, and for some unknown reason, sports a crazy beard! He always brings levity to any situation. *

Sunday, September 27th Caregiver Barbara (his mom)

"BP 127/70- Looking good! Talking with the nurses. Sitting, talked, and showered before I got here. Magnesium drip. Very alert and sharp. Did not nap in the morning. He ate lunch and then put his head down to sleep. Dr in. Dan asked for a protein drink. Dr totally in favor. Starting with dinner - but Gabby, his then nurse, brought him Boost right away. He said it was good. He is on blood pressure medications."

*Interjection: Many medications cause high blood pressure, so he was prescribed one to control his blood pressure. *

Monday, September 28th, Caregiver Sue (wife)

I got here at 7:00 am. Dan had blood in his urine last night, but all was clear and normal when tested overnight. He has a drip of saline and Magnesium. 7:00 am, changing of the nurses. BP127/67. Still dealing with diarrhea. I asked Colleen if she could order Tucks for soothing. Came up quickly. He slept all morning. Walked 3 laps. But really hates to walk. He chatted on the phone and walked another 3 laps. His sugar level was good, but his BP dropped, causing him to feel lightheaded. 2nd shot of Methotrexate, which is his anti-rejection drug. Brutal on him."

Tuesday, September 29th Caregiver Sue (wife)
"Arrived at 6:15.

Rough night. Felt nauseous. He did not throw up.

I brought Brendon's "Grandpops Happy Board" cards and notes from friends and family. He liked looking at it.

Slept most of the day. Not eating or drinking enough.

Weight-Lost 3 ½ pounds. Took nausea medicine, but it made him tired. I helped him shower. He sometimes fights me on taking a shower but always thanks me and says he feels better. BP steady at around 130/89. Hemoglobin 6.1 had an infusion. Should not go below 7. This is not a worry since it was expected."

Wednesday, September 30th Caregiver Sue (wife)

"He had another rough night. Bouts of diarrhea and hard stools are causing most of his angst. It seems to be either/or. He is getting increasingly anxious about the bathroom. BP 127/ something. He was eating well, trying to order high protein meals with high fats: butter, bacon, and fattier cuts of meat. The nurse Practitioner asked him if he wanted another unit of blood since he was only at 7, but he said no. He is starting to push back a bit. Walked 4 laps. PT was with him. He showered and napped. Note to next caregiver, might need to order more Tucks for him…running low. I stocked up on bathroom toiletries; he will have enough till I come back on Monday."

Thursday, October 1ˢᵗ Caregiver Dayna (sister)

"On a hemoglobin drip when I arrived. Also, a magnesium drip. He says he is bouncing between constipation and diarrhea. Trying to get him to drink more water. He said he worked out in the room this morning and showered before I arrived. Had lunch before noon. (Mag. Drip goes until 2:30 pm) Alert, comfortable, no signs of nausea. Did have some pressure/congestion in sinuses overnight, fine for now BP 130/78. After nap & drip finished, 4 laps, and a cup of coffee (not in that order!), (he is) Anxiously awaiting Day 6 slime. (methotrexate)

4:25 BP 144/83. Methotrexate stomach injection during dinner. Dan wanted me to note that he sat in the chair for an hour after walking. ☺ He remembers to brush his teeth and gargle after each meal. He forgot to wear gloves when he went out for a walk.

Please note that he will not always say what he means to the nurses or doctors. He is aware of the consequences. Tim, have a good day." (Changed to Nicholas)

Friday, October 2ⁿᵈ Caregiver Nicholas (son)

"Arrived at 7:30 am. Soo, the nurse will give dad pain medication for his butt pain issue. She also ordered Cortisone cream. 8:00 am Dad, and I took a 10ish minute walk, 3 laps. 8:38 am Nurse said his red blood cells are at 6.9, so they will give him a bag of blood. They want his blood to be above 7. A Magnesium bag as well. BP 123/75, 98 heart rate, Oxygen 97% Temperature 97.9 - 8:44am. No more injections in the belly. BP 127/75- 10:00 am Started Magnesium and Blood drip simultaneously. BP 132/79-10:30am. 12:30 BP 138/81 Heart rate 92. At 3:10 Dad and I took 3 more laps. 3:48 Nutritionist said to drink a Boost if dad does not feel like eating his meal. He will be back early next week."

*Interjection:

Nicholas is our 3rd born son and last. He is not married. He is quiet and reflective. He is like his dad with his zeal for history and travel, which gives them hours of subjects to talk about. Nicholas never asks questions when situations arise; he is always ready to help. He is our family's go-to guy. After selling our house in 2014, we were not prepared for our "forever home," and Nicholas was tired of paying rent. We purchased a house together in 2015, 7 months before Dan's cardiologist appointment. *

Saturday, October 3rd Caregiver Eric (son)

"BP 120/69. Dad walked one lap. Dad is tired and has very loose stool. He's gone poop 3 times since I've been here. The nurse says he is not drinking enough water. Otherwise, he seems to be doing well. Blood was drawn to check magnesium; the nurse said low levels."

*Interjection: Drinking water and walking. My nemesis with my husband. He is so good in many ways, but, man, oh man, the guy will not drink or walk enough. Walking is essential to help the natural physical decline during a hospital recovery. "Water hurts my stomach and tastes nasty." His sister bought him lemon water; I bought him packets that go in bottled water. Neither worked. When he walks, everyone can hear because he scuffs his feet along the ground, like a 4-year-old who will not tie his shoes. One day one of the nurses put a sign on the floor for him to pick his feet up. Hahaha, he thought it was funny… He has been doing that for years. No reason. The nurses all love him. One sat with him to watch football during his break. They all tell me he is their favorite! But that water and walking thing, he is not mine in that! *

Grandpa's Happy Board

Brendon, at the time 7 years old, Eric and Elise's eldest, created a special board for Grandpop. He said, "When Grandpop looked at the board, he would be happy" All the grandchildren added their own touch.(Hayleigh, Bryce, Alyson, and Aubrey. Nolan wasn't born yet.) In Dan's room was a corkboard on the wall near his window, which I deco-rated with well wishes and pictures from friends and family. I later added his birthday cards.

At our home, my daughter-in-love, Elise, could organize an organizer. Elise and her sister Brittany completed the rest of the house set-up for Dan's return home while I was at the hospital, visiting my parents, or working. Eric and Elise lived in their RV with two boys (one on the way). They are Global Relief Missionaries in the USA and take their home with them wherever they go. During COVID-19, Campgrounds were closed, so they left PA and parked in our driveway. They ended up being a blessing to Dan and me. Such a huge help getting the final touches finished and cleaning accomplished before he came home.

Everyone asked me how I was doing. I did not know how to answer. I was not focused on myself. I did what I had to do and moved on. I did not know, but I was doing okay. Yes, of course, it was horrible. Yes, I was incredibly sad, scared, and hurt watching my husband get stuck with countless needles and watch him struggle. There have been other times in my life it was hard; one of my sons almost died at birth and then two more times during his life. So, if you asked, I did not know how to answer, except I kept it honest and let it flow. I let my emotions fly at Ana's funeral. A brief moment of relief.

The hospital stay for Dan's Allogeneic Stem Cell Transplant was eye-opening. Nurses were very upbeat, kind, and genuinely concerned about him. I was not happy with the constant changing of the nursing staff. Usually, we would have the same nurse for three days, then a new nurse. We never had the same nurse for more than three days. I thought that was detrimental to him. He would have to answer the same questions each time, and it would take at least a day to have them understand him. Important to access, I think. Not clinically, but knowing how he is; breathing sounds he makes when moving vs. sounds indicating he was short of breath, not hanging all the IV bags simultaneously, so he was not tethered 24/7, having to explain his bathroom problems, etc. If it were the same nurse, it would have been easier. Same with the night nurse.

They also could not agree if he could have coffee from the machine in the nurse's kitchen or only from the Main hospital kitchen... I worked in a Dining Room setting, and well, it's the same thing. (The thought was the kitchen machines were cleaned often, thus fewer bacteria build-up). They both use machines. Also, it has been my experience that the carafes they use from the Main Kitchens are not cleaned very often. I know this sounds like a minimal concern considering everything else. However, it takes everything away from you, including energy, and becomes more arduous. Bacteria has become a legitimate concern! Besides, the Main Kitchen consistently forgot his coffee. It quickly became no caffeine anyway.

Father and Daughter

During this time, my father was not doing well. The last time he was coherent enough to have a daughter-dad conversation, I asked him to keep fighting. I told him I needed him; Dan was so sick…do not leave me! He told me he would try, and Dan would be okay! My father is an interesting combination of impatience and soft-heartedness. My father had an alcohol problem when I was younger. He was not a mean drinker, and I do not recall him ever being drunk, but I know he was not present in those moments. He used to lay on the floor in front of the tv to have better access to channel changing.… I lay on the other side just to be with him.

He was an "over the road" truck driver for a few years, and when he was gone, I missed him. One of my fond memories is playing softball with the neighborhood kids in the backyard. As he grew older, he could not play anymore but would coach a men's softball team. I would help with the score sheet when needed. I was a bit of a klutz, and I still am. But I grew to love watching football and played the best I could in softball. When I was eight, my father started going to church with us and gave his heart to the Lord. He never drank alcohol again. For many years my father blessed his grandchildren, showering them with love. He would work all night, then pick up doughnuts and milk to surprise those who lived close by. He was my go-to for driving, emergency grocery trips, doctor appointments for the kids, and anything else I needed. He would be there. Once Nicholas was stung by several underground hornets and was laboring to breathe, he drove us to the hospital. As he became older, he got more annoyed with things, but he always was available for family!

My brother Rick and his wife Nikki gave up work time to help mom and dad in any way possible. Nikki helped dad with medication, appointments and shopped for food for them. Rick maintained maintenance on the home.

My brother Bill and his wife Eileen, (NJ) collaborated with the doctors for Dad's care. After a while, my brother Ernie took over that responsibility. Ernie (Iowa), my sister Kathy (Texas), and my niece Rebecca (Iowa) stayed with mom while dad was in the hospital or rehab or his few days at home. What a wonderful gift they all were. He would get a bit better, but then he would decline. He wanted to be able to take care of mom again. He was losing his will and his battle.

Back to Logbook
Sunday, October 4th Caregiver Barbara (his mom)

"Very weak when I arrived but pushed himself to walk one lap. BP 120/71- Perfect. They hooked him up with 3 drip lines: blood transfusion, magnesium, and saline. It only took two hours.

He showered after he had walked earlier. Slept a little. He did not eat all his lunch but drank a Boost. Walked 2 laps after lunch. He needs to eat less starch + more vegetable and fruit and fruit juices! No wonder he is having trouble with elimination! He says he feels much better than he did earlier. BP 145/81- Jessica says because of pressure from transfusion."

*Interjection — Parking and Traffic –

I hated driving into Philly on Mondays and Fridays. Traffic began to back up on the NJ side over the Walt Whitman Bridge, going into Philadelphia around 7:30 a.m. Traffic was not the problem; it was the crazy peeps who thought it was okay to weave in and out and do it poorly. There were times I would get to the hospital shaking. I like to drive; I can drive; I just do not like risking my life!

Construction…my other nemesis. I swear that every road I was on was under construction. Always an added exciting element. If I arrived around 10:00 a.m., the Perelman parking lot was full. I just rode around until it opened, or, one time, I had to valet park the car. (Before that was shut down because of COVID). It cost $11 each day to park; the bridge toll was $5; food average was $8. We gave each of our kids a credit card when they were the caregivers so they wouldn't incur a cost. Dan's mom would get dropped off at the front lobby. Low-cost parking ($5) at HUP was two blocks away from the hospital at Building 3600. On the hospital campus, a shuttle ran between 3600 and other buildings, including HUP. Other caregivers would park there, but I left the hospital at night and did not feel safe walking to 3600 or taking the shuttle.

Dan was hospitalized during the BLM protests; at times, the University of Pennsylvania was experiencing active demonstrations. One night right near 3600, something was going on. Five police cars. Not the night for a stroll.

I would wake up and leave home most days by 5:30 a.m. to get a parking spot and avoid the problems. It was starting to take a toll on me. I was with Dan for 10-12 hours, three days a week, working four days and helping my parents as best I could. On top of that, I watched my husband begin the struggle for his life. Thank you, Lord, for a big supportive family. But that traffic! *

Monday, October 5th Caregiver Sue (wife)

"Arrived at 7:30 am

Hemoglobin 6.4, getting an infusion. Nurses reassured us this was normal in the process. BP 143/83. I helped him shower and noticed a rash on his back; I took a picture and showed the nurse. The Team ordered cream Nystatin and Triamcinolone."

*Interjection: Showers remove the drugs that are excreted through the skin. There were times that I walked into his room and smelled garlic. That was the medication coming out of his skin. During our class before Dan's SCT, the nurse practitioner emphasized the importance of showers and staying clean of germs. Showers were becoming harder for him, and it was just too much one day!

Horrible shower time! Horrible! He was trembling so badly; it was hard to get him washed. I was crying and wet, and he was miserable and cold, and I learned an important lesson; listen to him! Half a shower was better than none. I allowed my need to be the best caregiver to overtake my need to hear, which is crucial. There were times my task was unrealistic. I needed to take a breath and realize I had never been in this situation before. Neither of us had. I was becoming overly clinical and leaving out the humanity. *

"Took 2 laps after platelets were infused around 3 pm. He is not 3 eating much: crackers and muscle milk."

Tuesday, October 6th Caregiver Sue (wife)

"Arrived7:15 am

BP 130/.75 He is getting weaker. He has mouth sores and a throat ache, saline drip, 3 laps, magnesium drip (2 a day), took his usual pills, last day for methotrexate injected 5:00.

Caregivers- I am consistently sharing with nurses what Dan won't share. He is afraid that it will never stop once he starts medication for his concerns, diarrhea, rash, mouth pain, etc. Access him when you come in, see something, and share with staff so they can talk with him. He did not want anything for his mouth sores or the pain. But I spoke to the nurse on duty, and she was able to talk him into trying the medication; he said it helped. Ice chips are on the freezer door.

Showered. It was a busy day with Team members checking in. He is in pain, butt hurts, but ate better today."

Wednesday, October 7th Caregiver Sue (wife)

"8:00 am Temp 98.4 BP 136/81; he ate some oatmeal, pears, and coffee.

Lunch: all soft food. Hard for him to walk with swelling in both ankles, so no laps. Hopefully, it will be better tomorrow. The Tacrolimus and Magnesium are causing the trembling. Too much or too little of one or the other is causing the concerns. He sits in the chair, but not often.

Neupogen and Zarxio injections were given at bedtime to raise his white cell count.

More pain meds at lunch and bedtime. I have been pushing the pain meds, and it is helping. Oxy is not good. It caused him to have bad dreams that seemed like he was awake. He said no more of that! Doubled the other pain meds."

Thursday, October 8th Caregiver Dayna (sister)

Dan is pretty wiped out today. It's hard for him to eat because his throat is so sore. His spirits are okay, but I think he is trying because I'm here. He ate little lunch, but he managed to have some of the apple crisp I brought him. I didn't arrive until 11:00 am; he had only walked up and down the hall once, he said. His hair is starting to fall out. Feet elevated to help with the swelling he noticed yesterday. I reminded him to brush his teeth and gargle. (After drip was done, after lunch.) No magnesium drip yet today, but he is expecting it. Head floor nurse in twice without gloves on. It did not make me happy. Leora, student nurse-very friendly. Walked 2 complete laps- linen changed - showered- slept 2 to 4 hours. P.S. No Imodium today - was okay with bowel movements but had a sore bottom. The back rash appears to be clearing up. Dan mentioned there were 16-17 people in the room (in and out) this morning. 4:00 pm

BP 118/70. I bored Dan with my Witch's House story before I headed out. Xoxo, I Love you guys!"

*Interjection:

During October, Dan's sister is employed at a farm where she entertains as a storytelling witch. She writes her own stories and likes to try them out on family members. Dan was a captive audience *

Friday through Sunday, October 9th through 11th
Caregiver Sue (wife)

"These days were uneventful, except for his shave. The rash on his back was healing nicely. Swelling in ankles down."

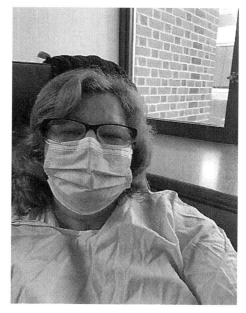

One of my visiting days!

Time to Shave

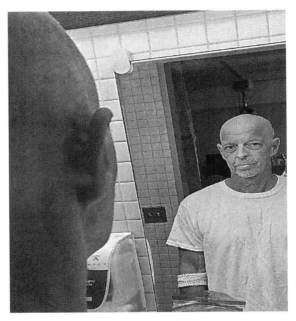

Dr. Mary Ellen from the rounds Team noticed Dan was losing hair. "Time to shave his head. No sense getting all that hair stuck on sheets." I borrowed Wahl Clippers from the nurse's station (sadly, it is a staple,) and we went to the bathroom for a shower and shave. I ensured the room was warm by turning on the shower before he came in. He was starting to complain about his back. I think it was because he was in bed for too long. Once the hair shaving was finished, we stared in the mirror at his reflection for a few seconds without saying anything. With tears in his eyes, he said, "I never really believed I had cancer 'til now." I hugged him. "No, you are beating cancer, and this is what the fight looks like." He smiled. "Yeah." I grabbed my phone and captured the essence of the truth in the quiet, motionless picture.

Logbook Continued
Monday, October 12th Caregiver Sue (wife)

"Dr. Mary Ellen came in at 9:00 am; Dan is coming home! His ANC went up. (The absolute neutrophil count estimates the body's ability to fight infections, especially bacterial infections.) I am gathering most of his items from his room and heading home for the final preparation! Excited but anxious as well. Stopped working on October 11th, ready!"

Tuesday, October 13th Discharge Caregiver Sue (wife)

I arrived at 8:00 am. Both of us were nervous. Thank you, caregivers!

Tramadol for his back pain. Mouth sores are much better. BP and pulse ox look good. Pharmacy came to the room with home medication instructions, and the nurse gave us the discharge papers and told us about his next visit to Penn. They gave him 1 unit of blood, saline drip, and magnesium drip before we went. The social worker also came by; Penn Home Infusion Nurse will begin at our home tomorrow. Lots of phone numbers in my book."

A Moment of Levity

Transport wheeled him to Perelman Connector. He said he could not take Dan to the car because the parking garage was in the Perelman Center, another building. There is a connecting walkway between buildings. Dan had to walk the rest of the way. I was not happy about that. (In the future, I brought up a wheelchair when he was discharged.) Dan was looking out the windows of the connector walkway like a little kid being outside after a long day cooped up! While we were waiting for the elevator, a guy asked us to move up so he could go down the stair (door behind us). Dan was an ill patient, and though we moved up a little, this guy walked past and said, "Well, I guess three feet will have to do." Very rude. COVID-19 made people lose their minds and their humanity. Or maybe it was just the big-city attitude. We had our masks on. Made us both laugh at the ridiculousness. Dan opened the window to feel the outside air as we drove home. I will never know exactly what he went through. I am amazed by his strength. I looked at him and saw he had lost weight and had physically changed. The home battle had begun.

Chart following his cells transformation

Name D.H.
Rm:

DAILY BLOOD COUNT RECORD

DATE	Day (+/-)	WBC (thousand)	ANC	Hgb (gm/dl)	PLT	TRANSFUSIONS
9/18	-7	35.0		7.8	370	Ø
9/19	-6	28.8	20,740	7.6	345	Ø
9/20	-5	31.2		8.3	353	Ø
9/21	-4	32.4	23090	8.6	343	Ø
9/22	-3	22.2		7.5	332	Ø
9/23	-2	20.0	17490	8.3	306	Ø
9/24	-1	10.1	10,880	8.5	306	Ø
9/25	0	3.7	3,030	8.1	278	cells!
9/26	1	2.2	2100	7.7	241	
9/27	2	1.4	1200	7.6	239	
9/28	3	1.1	900	7.5	212	
9/29	4	0.9	850	6.1	167	
9/30	+5	0.8	690	7.0	144	
10/1	+6	0.7	590	6.7	85	
10/2	+7	0.6	550	6.9	53	
10/3	+8	0.6	310	7.1	31	
10/4	+9	0.4	240	6.6	15	1 RBC
10/5	+10	0.3		6.6	8	1u Plt + 1u RBC
10/6	+11	0.4		7.0	10	Ø
10/7	+12	0.3	150	7.2	9	Ø
10/8	+13	0.6	490	6.9	10	
10/9	+14	0.7	550	7.7	17	
10/10	+15	0.7	490	7.3	23	

(-) days are those before transplant; (day 0) day of transplant; (+) days begin after transplant day or on day 1 of chemo in non-transplant patients

Normal Values:
WBC (White Blood Count): 4-10 (thousand)
ANC (Absolute Neutrophil Count):
    <500= neutropenia-severe risk for infection
    <1000= neutropenia- increased risk for infection
    <1500= normal risk of infection
Hgb (Hemoglobin):   Male 14-18
                     Female 12-16
                     Elderly (slightly lower)
PLT (Platelets): 150K-300K

Transfusion Parameters:
Hbg < 8 → 2 Units of blood
PLTS < 10K → 6 Units of platelets

* Transfusions may vary based on individual patient needs

hemoglobin: <7= be careful w/ m
platelets: <50= no resistance
          <10 = light activity

HOME HEALTH CARE

*"To know even one life has breathed easier
because you have lived, that is to have succeeded."*

-Ralph Waldo Emerson-

CHAPTER 9

WAS READY WITH the proper foods, cleaning products, and extra linen for his daily bed changes. Penn Home Infusion delivered the magnesium bags and supplies the day we came home. Erin stopped by to see if I could use any help. She took one look at the number of delivered supplies and headed to Target. She came back with a four-tiered cart and set it up. Yes! Tubes, alcohol wipes, flushes, lines, a machine that broke down the blood for testing, an IV pole, twelve medication bottles, two pumps with bags, all that goes with it, and more. It was organized and ready.

After my brother Ernie left to go back to Iowa, my mom stayed with us. She was surprised by how much there was to do. Erin helped with the initial setup of the pill dispenser with me. Fourteen pills, two IVs. She and I fol-lowed the instructions and added his drugs to the correct day dispenser, morning, afternoon, and evening. This part was so important to get right! It took time to get used to and feel con-fident with the system. I knew I was sometimes tired and did not want to miss or mess up anything. When his weekly pills were set up in a dispenser, I had another person work with me.

Our Penn Home nurse, Amanda taught me the backpack pump for his IVs, flushes, and injection routines. I had this! Amanda came back the next day to make sure I was good. Dan was still having trouble with his back, but he could come out to the kitchen and watch while I went through training. After taking his vitals, he returned to his room and laid back down. I thought it was tiredness from the trip home from the hospital. Amanda said she would come the next day if needed, but I was good for a few days.

His back problem persisted, so his Team placed him on pain meds every four hours. I talked him into a warm bath, hoping his back would feel better. Not a great idea. Nicholas was home by then and had to help get him out. I contacted Dan's medical team, and they upped his pain medication. I was concerned.

Each day the pain seemed to worsen. The pain reliever was not helping, so I spoke to his Team late Friday. There was no fever, so they said to add warm compresses and wait until the nurse checked him on Monday.

He could barely move. He was in so much pain. I slept in the chair in his room to comfort him and me. On Monday, October 19th, the home nurse took one look at him, took his vitals, called the doctor, and told him to go to the Emergency Room at The Hospital of the University of Penn.

It was a horrible ride for him. He was in so much pain. It broke my heart. There is a little parking area in front of ER that fits one car; through God's grace, it was open. A security guard came out, helped get him into a wheelchair, took him in, and I went back out to park the car. I was unhappy with him sitting in the ER waiting room since he was susceptible to infections. COVID-19 was extremely high, and he was sick and in excruciating pain. I contacted his doctor at Pearlman Center (adjacent to the hospital) to see if they could get him out of the ER waiting area and into an ER room faster for Dan's safety. They made it work. From 10:30 a.m. until the following day, he stayed in a private room in the emergency department. There were no rooms available in Rhodes 7. I was not happy with the ER. It was not clean. I cleaned the room myself and was very annoyed that the nurses did not use alcohol wipes before flushes. I am not a mean person; I just wanted him to be safe! Just the basics. Dan did not like me to make waves, so I made ripples and kept my man safe.

Diagnosis: pneumonia and spinal abscess, which likely started before he left the hospital. He never had a chance. We credit Amanda for saving his life! Dr. Mary Ellen said that Dan had a few hours or a day, and we would have lost him. He was holding the hem of Jesus's garment.

He was wheeled back onto the floor he had left just days ago; it was so sad. It was nice to see familiar faces but discouraging. He was on two strong antibiotics in the ER. Vancomycin, and every 12 hours Cefepime. His Team of doctors thought it best to begin giving it to him. Next, a Spine Biopsy was scheduled to determine what kind of bacteria caused the abscess and pneumonia and help target treatment. Unfortunately, the sample could not give them the information since the antibiotics were already clouding the bacteria. So, instead of a one-to-two-week antibiotic treatment, it turned into six weeks.

In the hospital, managing his pain was through Tramadol. He did take oxycodone during this second stay, and it gave him the first relief he had, and he could sleep. Unfortunately, it gave him horrible nightmares again. I went in as early as possible and stayed until they kicked me out. He would look at me when I went in, and I could see him relax. During this stay, he was starting to develop a bit of confusion, or what is called "hospital psychosis." It is a common condition for those in the hospital for a long time. It was not a bad case, but I made sure I was there for 12 hours every day. I hated leaving him. If it were not for COVID-19, I could have stayed all night, although my mom also needed me. Rick and Nikki hired a woman to take mom back and forth to the hospital to see dad during the week, and friends and family would take her on the weekend.

My Father

By Thursday, October 22nd, a decision had to be made about my dad. He was not getting better at Virtua Garden State Rehab in Marlton, NJ. He would not be able to come home, and rehab wanted him to be discharged. My mom could not take care of him at home, and we had exhausted all the siblings and family members that could help.

On Friday, October 23rd, I drove mom to the rehab and met with a Palliative Care Representative. My brother Ernie set up a Facebook room for the rest of my siblings so they could hear and help mom with any questions she might have. My dad woke and looked at me and said to the representative, "everyone needs a Susie in their lives." I write that because that was the last time I heard my father's voice, and it was beautiful for a daughter to hear. I was going through so much with Dan; Dad made it all better. I tried to be strong enough, but sometimes I was running on empty.

The Palliative Care Representative tried to ask my father what he wanted and where he wanted to go, but Dad fell asleep. His carbon dioxide levels were deficient, and his organs were struggling. He explained to Mom Dad's options, Hospice, home, or a Palliative Care facility. Hospice would mean he was com-ing home, but it was not an option with my hands full with Dan, other family members working full-time, and dad's level of care. A skilled care nursing facility was the best option. Mom kept looking at dad to help her with such incredible sadness. She sat there wringing her arthritic hands, trying to stay calm and yet, not wanting to make a choice. She had to go home and think. Mom was 86 years old; they had been married for 63 years.

Also, on Friday, Dan's PICC Line stopped working. They brought the X-ray machine to his room, and yes, the PICC line had to be changed. It was a Friday. We had to wait until Monday! As is the way in all hospitals, everyone but the surgeon works on the weekend. EVERYONE! The nurse had to place two intravenous lines in Dan's hand until his PICC line was changed. He said they burned a little, but he was still on pain medication, which helped. Nicholas stayed with Dan on Friday; Eric remained on Sunday.

On Sunday, October 25th, through prayer and talking with the siblings, Mom decided skilled care nursing was the only option. Mom and my sister-in-law Nikki went in to sign the papers for dad to be moved to Samaritan Center in Voorhees, NJ, later that day. No more awful tests. No more forcing the air mask on him that rubbed his nose raw. My father was expected to last just a few weeks or less. But mom was optimistic he would get better. Dad was loaded into an ambulance around 7 pm. Nikki drove Mom behind the ambulance that took him to his last home on earth. Mom said it was a beautiful facility. He asked why he was there and settled in for the night. Mom tucked him in, and he kissed mom two times. He wondered what her plans were because he never liked her home alone, and she said, "I'm staying with Susie." He said, "Good." She left after he fell asleep, exhausted. She would be able to spend the night with him now. She slept well that night. God gives us strength even when we do not know we will need it. As would our family, she would need it over the coming days.

Ceal Christy- Foster (Aunt) took this picture of Dad a few
years before he died. He said he always wanted it to be an obit-
uary picture
…it was.

HOMECOMING TAKE #2
&
MY FATHER

"The righteous man walks in his integrity;
His children are blessed after him."

-Proverbs 20:7-

CHAPTER 10

O N MONDAY AT 8:00 a.m., Dan was in the operating room. At 8:30 a.m. I received a call from my sister-in-law, Nikki, that Palliative Care had called because Dad had a rough night and was sedated twice and would make it through the day, but we better get Mom there. I was in Philly, Nikki and Rick lived in Langhorne, PA, and the rest of the siblings lived even further away. I called my sons Tim and Nicholas (they work for the same company) 20 minutes from our home. Nicholas was able to leave work. I should have called my mom to be ready. I should have told her Nicholas was coming to take her to see dad. They lost precious minutes. She was so fragile I did not want to scare her without someone being with her. He picked up mom and got her to Samaritan Hospice 15 minutes from my house. They did not make it in time.

I saw Dan's Team doing their rounds in the hospital corridor and asked if we could speed the discharge up; I needed to be with Dad. I explained he did not have time left. They immediately went into overdrive to speed up the pharmacy and discharge papers. The pharmacy came to instruct me on his new medications, and his nurse gave me his discharge papers. Transport had just brought Dan back into the room when I got the call I dreaded; Dad had passed. With a room full of nurses, I sobbed in the corner of the room, looking out the window. Dan later told me it broke his heart that he could not hold me.

I wanted to be with Mom. I wanted to hold her and

comfort her. Why was I not able to be in two places at once? I was so very thankful, again, for strong family members. But I lost my dad, and I could not say goodbye.

The drive home was so sad—what a mix of emotions. My husband was going to be okay; my father was not. My mom needed me. My husband needed me. Through God's grace, through God's love, through God's strength, I made it through. I will never know how he brought me through, but He did.

October 27th
Weight– 160lb 3.2oz
Body Mass Index 24.56

On Monday, October 26th, Dan would come home with two extra IVs and 24 pills per day. Again, up for the task, Rachel (Nicholas's girlfriend) helped set up pills. I requested Dan come home with the IVs instead of the antibiotic pill form since it was easier on his stomach. Dan's care tripled. Along with the other medications from before, and since the antibiotics were not compatible, my schedule consisted of getting up by 6:30 a.m. to change his IVs and going to bed by midnight when his last IV was finished for the night. My life became hard between making the right food, administering pills in the morning, afternoon, and evening, cleaning his room and bathroom daily, and trying to comfort my mom.

Folks offered to help. I was not alone, but I was alone. Of course, the caregiver, daughter, and wife in me did what I needed to do. I have often said that I will have a nervous breakdown as soon as I have the time. Silly, but silly sometimes brought me through.

Funeral

I had set up a Facebook page for updates on Dan's condition for family and close friends, "Prayers for Dan." I reached out to my "Prayers for Dan" group now to see if someone felt comfortable enough to stay with Dan so I could go to my father's funeral. He could not be left alone. My cousin Wade and his wife Lisa, two amazing folks, offered. I was very thankful! They both were away from the virus areas and worked their jobs alone. Dan would need an IV change, and they were more than willing. What a blessing!

I was asked if I wanted to say a few words at the funeral. I wanted to. I wanted to share with folks how much my father meant to me, to honor him. I just could not. I was very fragile at that moment; I knew my limits. My brother Ernie was the service pastor. He brought humor and remembrance. Our son Eric spoke on behalf of Dad's grandchildren and great-grand-children, many of whom were there. He said of Pop-pop's giving heart and shared their cherished stories. I wished Dan could have heard his son talk about the great man my father was. Dan wanted to be there, but it was not possible. My father would have said, "Let the man be!"

Ernie ended the service with Mom's favorite hymn, "In the Garden," and a prayer. My brothers paid for a light luncheon at mom and dad's church. I video-called Dan so he could say hello to the out-of-town guests. It was a strange moment in time, hearing observations like, "It doesn't look like Uncle Danny." I arrived home and spent time with Wade and Lisa, who spoke, "Dan did well. They are such a lovely couple. They sent Dan cards often and brought goodies for me. After they left, it was time to set up the next IV pump and administer medications. Grieve is placed in the back corner of my mind for now.

The next day, the family went to the cemetery to say our last goodbyes. Our son Tim offered to stay with Dan. At the last funeral, Tim also stayed with Dan, sweet Ana. The day was cold and damp, which cuts through gloves and coats. We sat in an outside pavilion that was being used because of COVID-19.

Nicholas, my mom, and I arrived at the Brigadier General William C. Doyle Memorial Veterans Cemetery 15 minutes before our motorcade headed to the pavilion. Family from all over the US were there. There was a beautiful flag ceremony, my brother Ernie spoke, and we all said our quiet goodbyes. Mom handed out the cards she ordered through the funeral director to each family member. We all quietly walked to our cars. I could not speak. I could not correctly thank the fantastic folks who stood by dad for so long. I just breathed. And I watched mom. Nicholas never left her side. My hero, my father, was gone. I looked at my family members wanting to say something, wanted to give comfort to the pain I saw in their eyes, but my pain was overwhelming.

Very few times in life, you see someone's actual pain. I sat in the back of the car, behind my mother in the front passenger's seat, as Nicholas drove away, heading to my mom and dad's house. I saw my mother's reflection in the passenger-side mirror, and the pain was unlike I had ever witnessed! This strong, brave, and kind woman, who had beaten down so many obstacles, found her Achilles heel. My heart ached for her. Even though we were with her, she was all alone. She just left behind her life. Was this my future?

Pulling up Strength

For the next few days, I sensed something was wrong with Dan. His appetite was not particularly good, and he complained of stomach pain. Residual from the last hospital stay, maybe? No fever, just pain, and he struggled with bowel problems. I contacted the Team, and they upped his Imodium. "It could be from medications." He took Ursodiol, two antibiotics, a magnesium drip, and tacrolimus; all can cause gut concerns. Great!

We had a new home nurse, Meghan; she would come every Monday and Friday. We had a Video Telehealth call with Dr. Elizabeth. Dan was eating cereal (one of the only things he could eat without pain, with a little lactose-free milk); she was happy to see he was eating. Could it be the medication, I asked. She thought it could be and lowered his Bactrim dose and increased his Imodium again. She was always very helpful and comforting.

I did not sleep in the same room as my husband for fear of germs. We re-did several rooms in the house to accommodate my mother and me before Dan went in for the SCT. We set up a camera in Dan's room to keep an eye on him and set up call bells in his room and bathroom. Best things ever! I highly recommend it! I was able to see him still sleeping and not go in and bother him. When he needed something, he pushed the button. It sounds like a doorbell! My mother-in-law thought she was cute by sending us a cowbell! Hahaha, nope!

I did not realize that my husband's fear of returning to the hospital was more significant than his concern for his welfare. He knew he was getting worse but kept the pain and how many times he had diarrhea to himself a day. He would tell me three times, but it was more like six times. I started to chart his bathroom issues. It was getting much worse.

Caregivers, taking notes will help you understand the patterns of your loved ones. When you are tired, retrieve the notebook, read and understand what the problem could be. Keeping this information will be a quick way to help answer doctors' questions, as well. This works with all care giving forms; food, bathroom issues, medication.

On Tuesday, November 3rd, I realized that he was getting in real trouble. I was keeping his Team informed through the message system at Mychartpenn. He had diarrhea every time he ate. He was losing more weight and not holding onto enough nutrients.

I stayed with him that night, sleeping in the chair in our room. I knew where we were heading and had to make the "call." I knew he would be upset. Again, not easy being a care-giver or wife. In the early morning, I contacted his care Team at Penn, he needed to go to the hospital. They were also moving in that direction. I got him dressed, packed what I thought he would need, including my crochet (not my first rodeo with ER), and headed to the Hospital of the University of Penn. My husband is a quick thinker; he grabbed a trash can and bags on the way out. He made it to Penn's parking garage, and he had to use the trashcan he brought as a bathroom. I was so upset for him; then I ran into Penn to use the bathroom myself. What a pair we were. When I got back, he thanked me for giving him some time; he was so embarrassed. Geez!

I had a wheelchair in the trunk of our SUV that I bor-rowed from a friend, Betty. I could not get one of the legs on, so Dan used the one-leg support, and I wheeled him to the ER. COVID-19 made its presence known. I could go to the tri-age room with him, which was good. I had to get someone to help him to the bathroom. He was so weak that it was hard to hold his head up. I held him until the doctor came in and said he was being admitted, but it would be some time before that happened because there were no available rooms. And to make it worse, the ER rooms were full as well. Security came into the triage room and told me that all visitors were being moved to the hospital's lobby. I looked at her with tears in my eye, this man, right here, you want me to leave? Yes. "They will come to get you when he has a room in the ER." "I'm so sorry, I wish we could do something, but tonight is really bad." He was so sad, so defeated. I told him he would be fine, kissed him on the head, and left to have my tears in the hallway. Dan has this strange ability to wrap himself in thoughts that take him away. He calls it a self-protection mechanism. Whatever it was, it helped him as he sat there alone.

I sat in the lobby while others were glued to Trump versus Biden's election. I pulled out my crochet, tucked myself in a corner so I could barely see or hear the TV, and worked on one of my "Warm Hugs by GiGi" blankets that I was making for each of my grandchildren. A security guard brought me to the waiting room five hours later, transporting us to an ER room. I looked at my husband, and he was so beat up. Five horrible hours. He had to use the bathroom several times by himself. How many others were here dealing with the same situation? There had to be a better way. How many people die trying to gain help through the ER? I, of course, again, cleaned his room in the ER the best I could. I even checked the bathroom he would have to use outside the room. The nurses were all over the place. Every bed was full, and you could hear the stress in their voices. "Too many COVID-19 concerns." "Short staffed."

Wednesday through Friday morning, he was in the ER. No room in Rhodes 7. Wednesday, I left at 7:00 p.m. so I could be back early. Thursday same thing, no room. Friday, he was heading to Dulles Wing, also an oncology floor. How he came through with his sanity intact is a mystery. He was given jello and crackers until he was admitted to the room, and then it was completely NPO. (Nothing by mouth)

Friday, November 6th
Weight – 140 lbs.

He lost 20 pounds in two weeks. He was exhausted. He stopped talking on the phone or texting with anyone, even his mother. He said even his fingers hurt. I kept everyone informed the best I could. Dr. Mary Ellen came in (the doctor from his first discharge), and she thought it was GVHD (Graft Vs. Host Disease) but would need a stomach and colon biopsy to be sure. She tried to get him in that day, but they were full. So, IT'S THE WEEKEND NOTHING GETS DONE! Ugh!

Over the weekend, they had him on NPO. He had not had any solid food. Medications were added to prepare for the biopsy, including cleaning out the colon, but it was not working. While I was on the phone with Dan's mom, she suggested an enema, and although he could not have a regular enema, he could have a water enema. The nurse came in twice. His body was producing so much of this black gooey stuff from his intestines; it worked, but not enough. Monday morning, two surgeons came in at 8:00 a.m. and told him they could not fit him in that day. When I arrived 10 minutes later, he told me what they said, and I went to the nurse's station and asked to speak to his Team. The Team was stunned as well. He was in for his biopsy within the hour. I was genuinely kind but livid inside. The surgeons were concerned they would not get a good look with all the dark goo and would be unable to get a sample; the Team said it was as good as they would get. It would take two to four days to have an answer. The Team started him on steroids on Friday just in case it was, in fact, GVHD. I asked many questions before starting the treatment, but not starting him on the steroids could have created a less desirable outcome.

Clinical Trial, Stage 3
Protocol N: Eq001–aGVHD–001
WCG Protocol #20182854
834123

Dr. Mary Ellen asked Dan if he would like to participate in a clinical trial for GVHD patients. The study used a medication given by IV at the start of GVHD to lower the risk of acute GVHD becoming chronic. His amazing Team heard Dan was coming to the ER with possible GVHD and put him on the list when there was just one opening. This began our introduction to another fantastic group of people, the Penn Research Study Team. I read Dan's research packet, gathered information online, and wrote my questions. We prayed, and Dan and I discussed it. He was willing to join the study. There are so many unknowns; faith is our friend.

The Toll on His Body

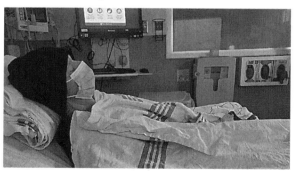

Dan in ER in November

Dan was changing before my eyes. Like a tree in the fall that slowly drops leaves that were so magnificent just a few months ago, he, too, was dramatically changing. He lost most of his body mass, and hair, and his skin was ashen. In the quiet moments, I questioned myself. Did I do everything right? Did

I clean, prepare foods, give correct medication, and use the flushes right? Did I cause this? Was I strong enough for one more day for the both of us? My car rides home were grief sessions or chatting on the phone with loved ones. It was okay to be not okay. Another lesson learned. The Lord would see me through; He would give me comfort. He would not judge me; He would love me, just as my earthly father did. It was okay. "Everyone needs a Susie in their life." I would be that for Dan!

My 10–12-hour visits were daily again. I asked if the caregivers could jump in on a Friday, Saturday, or Sunday to give me some time at home with Mom and have a break. The crazy elevator on Dulles felt like an experience from the Willy Wonka Chocolate Factory movie. It went so fast that you held on and just hoped it stopped on the sixth floor! My son, Eric, men-tioned it, as well. Oh, it is the little things that make one laugh.

Eating was complex. I was not allowed to leave the floor because of COVID-19, nor was I supposed to eat in the room or use the floor kitchen. I would wait until Dan fell asleep, eat under my mask, or go into the Nurse's kitchen and sneak a bite of crackers from their closet. I got caught a few times, but they were friendly and understood. It was great for losing weight. When Dan was awake, he watched the Food Network ALL DAY LONG. The nurses and I just laughed. He was still on a TPN bag (Total parenteral nutrition) of tricks for nutrition. Unfortunately, the nutrition bag raised his glucose, so out came the insulin shots and a prick on the finger every four hours. His arms and hands looked like pin cushions. There were so many bruises. He was very thankful for the PICC line for IVs.

His Attitude

Dan is such a nice guy. He was always kind to the staff. Even when he felt horrible, he was always kind. He let his "hair down" with me, as I am his soft place to fall. The staff all joked with him and spent extra time with him. I know they are trained to do that, but he was well-liked.

After five days on the TPN bag, the nutritionist allowed him to drink chicken broth. Dan was like a man who had not had anything for years! They introduced other foods: gelatin, pudding, soup, and decaf tea or coffee. I noticed they were giving him some items that had sugar or "broke down to sugar." Sugar can cause more diarrhea. I also noticed they started giving him Boost, which had dairy, another product that is hard to break down. The "Team" was a bit out of touch with the kitchen. The first time he could eat soup, they brought him tomato soup! I was not there to monitor that, and it made him sick. (Dan knew what he could and could not eat but assumed what he was given was okay.) The kitchen kept sending him regular coffee and tea with caffeine, which he couldn't have. I calledt he nutritionist, Ryan, and told him what was happening. He admitted it was a communication breakdown and would fix it. We never had another problem with the wrong food, but it had exacerbated his condition.

After a few days, the bowel concerns were getting worse again. He was back on "Nothing by Mouth" for four more days. The right foods were introduced slowly, starting with level GVHD 1 (jello, broths), then gently moving to level 2 (banana, toast). Dan was told to "eat slowly" over the day. Question: How were you supposed to slow down when they only brought food three times a day, and it was thrown out after an hour? Sigh. I started ordering more food, taking the extra off his tray, and storing it in the nurse's refrigerator. There were refrigerators in rooms on Rhodes but not on this floor. Although I stopped keeping a logbook, I texted the original caregiving Team to keep them informed. I overly texted; I'm sure most of them thought it was overdone, but they unknowingly were my lifeline.

PICC Line

The PICC line, again, is a wonderful invention. Dan was cautious with it, especially after the first change was needed, except one day, he quickly got out of bed in need of the bathroom and pulled it out about an inch from his arm. He forgot he was hooked up to the IVs. He was devastated! While he was in the bathroom, I pushed the call button. The nurse came in, shut off the pumps to the PICC line, and ordered an X-ray machine STAT to come to the room. It was one of the few times I saw Dan cry. His nurse again was wonderful. We calmed him, reassured him, and the X-ray showed it had moved but was okay. It did not have to be replaced!

The blood test we were waiting to get back was the Post-Transplant Chimerism. The test looks at the level of donor bone marrow versus the level of bone marrow from the patient (recipient). The CD3 (T-cells) and CD33/CD66 (Myeloid cells) began to tell the story. CD3 was 96% and CD33/CD66 was 27%. Overall BM 99%. The donor was trying, but the infections were making it hard. Dan started calling the female donor inside of him, "Viola." His blood type stayed the same. When it becomes mostly donor cells, his blood type will change to his donor's, A+.

Clinical Trial Begins/Ends

Dan had the first IV drip for the clinical trial on Thursday, November 12th. Did you ever have a niggly feeling, an instinct, that something was wrong? I could not say it was the Holy Spirit, but something did not sit right with me when it was going in Dan's veins. I could tell Dan felt the same. I feared this new drug, or maybe I had a gut feeling this was not a good idea. Or perhaps we were beaten up. Dan felt flushed and tired, but all went well as far as we knew. The clinical trial coordinator, Kim, stayed with Dan the whole time it was administered. She was a super friendly, funny gal. She drove Dan crazy with her chatter! He said she had way too much energy!

A few days later, his labs were terrible, although he was feeling much better. He was losing white and red cells dramatically. He was given an injection to boost his white cells, but they continued to drop. He was due for another round of clinical trial drugs, but I asked Kim to hold the drug when the research team came in. I was concerned it was what was causing it. They did not think it was the cause, but the drug was stopped to be on the safe side. After another Neoprene shot, he became stable. Unknowns are always the hardest to deal with, and best dealt through faith.

*Interjection:

We found out that one dose helped save Dan's life a few months later. *

Environmental Services

Dang! Dr. Mary Ellen was so mad the first time she saw the condition of the floor in his oom on Dulles that she requested as soon as possible to move Dan to Rhodes 7. Being an SCT patient and having GVHD was a cocktail for infection. A room on Rhodes never became available, which was okay with Dan. He liked the room on Dulles. It was quieter than Rhodes, but the cleaning was inconsistent.

We had one EVS worker who did an excellent job, but the rest, ugh! Every day, I cleaned surfaces that Dan would touch and made sure someone came to clean the bathroom and the floors. I had to clean the bathroom a few times. The bed changing was haphazard but was supposed to be done every day after his shower. I found the bed linen cart, changed the bed, and grabbed him clean towels. I did not mind helping and offered many times. Caleb, the boy wonder of EVS, was excellent. That room shined when he was done. But he did not work all the time. He brought over his manager, Barbara, to speak to me about my concerns.

Barbara worked Monday through Friday, again, (sigh) no weekends. Nothing changed. By the time I was there for three weeks, I had spoken to every "Team" member, social coordinator, and nurse that would listen. I had brought my portable air purifier and placed it in his bathroom by this time. The nurses were already annoyed with EVS. EVS had plenty of time to talk on their phones and chat in the hallways, just not enough cleaning time. They commented that they were short-staffed. Hmmm.

COVID-19 protocols were, kicking all visitors out on the upcoming weekend. I set up a meeting with Charles, another EVS manager, for the next day. I was kind, but through tears of frustration and fear, I explained that I was doing most of the cleaning unless Caleb was there (and he had mysteriously disappeared). I asked him to be my husband's advocate since I would not be in the hospital. My husband could die of a superficial infection.

He had a deer-in-the-headlights look, but thankfully Dan said his room was cleaned every day!

*Caregivers, never give up; you might find a brick wall

in the path, find a way to climb over. Be kind to those you encounter on the climb.*

MY SWEET MOM

In The Garden
I come to the garden alone,
While the dew is still on the roses
And the voice I hear, falling on my ear
The Son of God discloses
And He walks with me
And He talks with me
And He tells me I am His own
And the joy we share as we tarry there
None other has ever known

-Charles Austin Miles-

CHAPTER 11

Mom's vision is compromised. She had three strokes over ten years ago, which caused most of her eye problems and minor changes to her cognitive abilities. Dad did everything for mom; shopping, holding her hand while walking, and driving. Without him, she was not mobile outside of the home. My mom was alone while I was with Dan at the hospital. She was grieving and not eating well. While visiting Dan, my son called me on my cell phone, asking, "Can you be home with her more"? "Mom, she really needs you!" Dan began responding to treatment, and the kitchen concerns were fixed, so I felt comfortable changing my schedule. I did feel like I was being tugged in two different directions, but I love them both. I spent the mornings with mom and went to the hospital in the afternoon. Then Covid precautions started, and I was home with her for a week.

My mom and I are quite different. She has a place for everything in her house, while I am happy to open a closet and chuck things in. Dishes! I keep a pan in the sink and soak dishes that I do not get to immediately or for a day. It drove my mom crazy! Ha-Ha. "The dishwasher is right there!"

Of course, having your mom live with you brings up all the memories of the past...nothing terrible, just my household is set up with me in mind, not my mom! She helped by cleaning the dishes, sorting my kitchen drawers, and folding laundry. It was a tremendous help. My mom loves Dan! She has been one of his biggest cheerleaders and prayer warriors. "I pray for him every day," she said, "and before I go to bed at night!"

Dan and I would call each other, and I would prop the phone up and chat with him for hours while I worked on the "not so perfect" crochet gifts for Christmas. Mom would listen to her audio Kindle books and chat with Dan.

My mom and I worked together with the best we could. We needed the daughter/mother relationship, but neither of us could find our way there at times. I am an introvert, so going inside calms me. It helps me focus. Mom feels alone when her life is too quiet. Of course, the family wanted to help, but what could be done? Mom was feeling like a burden. I was feeling misunderstood. Life was just challenging.

Mom wanted to go home. She wanted to be where the memory of my dad was. Dad made it very clear she could not live by herself. The siblings talked about what to do. It was, of course, her life. Every morning mom would wake, cry, eat, and survive. I would wake, maybe eat, focus on getting Dan well, and try to make mom happy.

GoFundMe/Help

Dan's medical needs would be astronomical. It was ¾ of what his disability payments were. We had savings, but they would deplete quickly. Erin and Dayna set up a GoFundMe account to help offset medical, Insurance, and living expenses. It was an uncomfortable experience to have folks give us their hard-earned money. From our past acquaintances to our present, the donations came in! Dan's co-workers donated their Christmas holiday pay. My work gave us food and gift cards. Friends, family, and strangers donated. One of my favorite donations was from a little girl who donated $5, which spoke volumes about her heart and character.

We were in awe! Gifts, grocery cards, cash (anonymous gifts from church families), Wawa cards, and foods poured in. Neighbors brought over meals, and beautiful plants came by courier. It was all very humbling! We prayed each time we used any of the funds to ensure we honored those who donated. Our prayer is to be able to "pay back" and was given and to help others in their time of need. The stress that was released by their giving will never be forgotten. I would love to be able to mention them all, but God knows. May He bless them 10x10!

HOMECOMING TAKE #3

"I've learned that people will forget what you said, people will forget what you did, but people will never forget how you made them feel"

-Maya Angelou-

CHAPTER 12

Friday, December 4ᵀᴴ, he was coming home. Dan was brought out to the car by hospital transport, and off we went. We were emotionally and physically beaten up. He wanted a taco; I told him NO! Prednisone, a steroid, made him hungry, for which his Team and I were thankful. He was discharged without the two IV antibiotics, so he had a more straightforward medication routine. He slept most days in the bed in our room. I slept in the guest room again.

After two weeks, I was concerned that he was not coming out of the bedroom very often, and I needed to get him moving more. I cleaned the bedroom and bathroom daily (he had his own bathroom). He sat in the living room while I cleaned, then went back into the bedroom. I think he used it as a comfort area. I understood, but he needed to move more and get his mental state back on track.

Caregivers, this was the tricky part of the job. Making him move made him annoyed with me. But I knew his recovery would be stalled if he didn't move. Several times, I told him he could get mad at me, but he needed to move. Take a short walk around the inside or outside of the house. He did it but complained.

Penn Home Infusion visits began again, and it was Amanda. Virtua also sent out a nurse once a week. Amanda was professional and clicked with Dan.

Dan slept, ate, exercised, and watched TV for the next few weeks. He had anxiety when he came home that last time. Thirty-five days took a toll on him mentally. He experienced several rough nights with very horrible nightmares. I moved the chairs out of his bedroom and moved a twin bed in, so I could comfort him. He seemed to settle more with me sleeping in the room: or maybe I did.

It's hard to put into words what he went through, watching him suffer. It was heartbreaking. The amount of energy to accomplish the littlest tasks was huge. Getting a shower turned into his big event for the day. He would nap for a couple of hours afterward. The side effects from some of the Medications made it even harder for him to cope.

With Dan's GVHD, he was on a strict diet, and sometimes getting him to eat enough was challenging. "Drink, Drink, Eat, Eat" was my mantra. I knew dehydration was a threat, and nutrition was one of the keys to improving. But how far could I push? Far! I pushed it far and often. I did not care if he got annoyed. I promised him, in the beginning, that I would be his advocate in all areas, including against himself. We would cross the bridge of forgiveness after he got healthy. At that moment, we were in a fight for his life. Again, tricky business. I never yelled and kept my tone even, but I was firm.

Let's chat about the "diet." As stated before, we joined a required three-hour class before his SCT on Penn's Bluejeans. Eight other folks were going through SCT in this class or were the caregivers. I printed out the information they sent through e-mail into a three-ring bookbinder.

GVHD threw a wrench in the eating plan to make things more challenging. No dairy, no caffeine, no lettuce or fiber, no sugar, no red meats, no fruit except bananas, no, no, no. I consider myself an intelligent gal when it comes to cooking, but I often had to reach out to Elise to help me through this dilemma. He needed to have 1500-2000 calories a day. The GVHD also damaged his kidneys because of the weight he lost so quickly, and the TPN bag also damaged the "balance" of his minerals.

Homemade chicken broth and bone broths became a staple, with added vegetables on his list. I cooked low-sugar foods, non-dairy products, and homemade bread with nuts and dried fruit. My husband ate anything I put in front of him; he trusted that I gave him what he needed. I went to a health food store and chatted with the store associate, and we found a powder that would not hurt his creatine (which involves kidney function) but gave him the proteins and extra calories he needed.

Although it was complicated at first, after a week, it became routine. I spent funds from the generous donations on fish for Dan. He was supposed to have at least five servings per week. One of the Nutritionists at Penn, Ryan, and Elise recommended Wild Caught only, which increased the price.

Donor Update

The CD3 (T-cells) and CD33/CD66 (Myeloid cells). CD3 was 92% and CD33/CD66 was 38%. Overall BM 94%. The donor cells lost some ground.

Christmas was just around the corner. He was still having bouts of diarrhea, but it was controlled. We put up a small tabletop Christmas tree in the living room. None of us wanted to celebrate that year, but it felt good to have the joy of Christmas. It was a balance. One night when Dan was in the hospital, I came home to Christmas lights on the house. My mom said Nicholas knew it would make me happy. And it did!

My mom was sad Dad was not here, and I felt like I did not have my husband to lean on or my mom. But we would get through this as well. But I was feeling the cracks starting.

The constant cooking, cleaning, medication administration list, and organization were too much. I had become the all-around glue person. The trouble was that I was becoming unglued myself. Trivial things were making me angry, and I did not know why. I learned a lot about myself and my emotions. I thought I had it together. I had to stop trying to control everything because I did not know what the next day would bring. I always managed my environment, from homeschooling to hairdressing, to my home life. The situation was also complicated because I was alone for the first time in our marriage.

I could not go to Dan with my concerns or my fears. He needed me to fix them, not create them. My kids were getting concerned with the apparent cracks. They wanted me to see a counselor; I was not hiding it as well as I thought. I have my certificate in marriage and singles counseling. Funny how it is hard to help yourself.

Two positive changes were that mom wanted to try to stay at her house full time, and I decided to join a Women's Bible study on Zoom. Both became healing for us.

Being an introvert, bible studies with folks I didn't know always made me uncomfortable. I do not know if it was the distance of using Zoom or God's perfect timing, but it helped me. The stresses were still there, but I could compartmentalize them better. And I had ladies to talk about them with. I enjoyed it so much I started a zoom bible study after it ended.

Five ladies met every Tuesday night from 7 p.m. to 9 p.m. for six weeks. My sister Kathy joined in, which gave me great comfort. She is so funny, and when I struggled to explain myself, she jumped in and added clarity. This was also when Dan's mom started calling him every night at around 7:15 p.m. He loved talking to his mom; she helped him take his mind off his concerns, and the calls helped her. She lives in PA, and as I mentioned before, Dan's dad has Alzheimer's, and Barbara takes care of him at home.

Christmas 2020

Three days before Christmas, my mom and I drove out to visit dad's inurnment. Mom seemed to be doing better. She was doing well in her home environment. Everything was comfortable and familiar. There was a stand on the side of the road with Christmas wreaths, so I stopped and purchased one to place near dad's grave. It was a chilly day, and we did not stay long. I took a picture of mom sitting on the cold bench in front of Dad's inurnment. I wondered what she was thinking. I stayed quiet. Minutes passed, and she wiped her tears and said, "I think it is time to go." I had concerns about leaving the cemetery. The last time we had been there was his funeral. Would she feel like she was leaving him behind again? Would she feel that pain all over?

On the way home, she told me that Dad was not at the cemetery. He was in their shared home. Now I understood the change in mom. She was not crying as much and wanted to be home. God allowed that touch to help His child find peace and begin to work through her grief. Amazing grace!

Two weeks before Christmas, Eric and Elise took mom and me out (Dan stayed with Nicholas and Rachel) to a farm that set up a beautiful display of "drive-through" Christmas lights.

We had not seen our grandbaby boys for four months because of Dan's infection concerns. Although they had to stay at a distance with no hugs, it was wonderful to see them. Mom tried to enjoy what she could see, but the best part was doing something other than dealing with cancer and grieving. I was so thankful for that moment. I gave Eric's family their Christmas gifts and cried as they left the driveway to return home. I missed them and life. I poured my emotions into their homemade gifts; it was the best I could do.

Dan and I dropped off gifts for Tim, Erin, and our three grandbaby girls (5 miles away) on Christmas Eve. They all came outside and waved; no hugs again. I saw their bright little faces and heard them asking, "Why can't we hug Grandpop and GiGi?" Little ones do not understand the complexities of contagion. As we drove away, sadness invaded my heart. I won't dwell there for long, but the reality of being unable to hug my six grandchildren sat heavy. Family is one of the greatest gifts from God and should always be cherished.

Christmas was celebrated with my mom, Rachel, and Nicholas. My mother-in-law Barbara gave each family household an Echo Show from Amazon, and we were able to see our grandbabies open their gifts. That was incredibly special. I gave my mom a locket with my dad's picture inside; she wears it daily and his wedding ring around her neck. Sweet friends and family members made sure that our Christmas was special with gifts and calls.

New Year's Eve

I had not been able to "visit" my dad since his passing, alone. I wanted to be able to sit by his inurnment and talk. So, I went to the cemetery. I have found two kinds of folks, those who gain comfort in visiting their loved ones in cemeteries and those who do not. I receive comfort. Every new place I go, I try to check out the oldest cemetery, look up an old grave and tell them, "You are not forgotten." One day I will analyze why I do it, but for now, it brings peace.

The day was cold and rainy. It wasn't a downpour but a misty, foggy rain that makes your insides cold. There were two other cars where the columbarium was located, and yes, out of 12 rows, one family sat right in front of my dad's plaque. I waited on a bench on the side aisle, but it was too cold. I got back in my car, drove around for about 20 minutes, checked again, and the family was gone.

I stretched a cloth on the wet bench and began talking to my dad. I told him about Mom, Dan, my kids, and the grand-babies and asked for advice about an ongoing family concern. Mostly I just talked to my father, daddy-and-daughter style. An hour went by quickly, and it was time to go home. Nicholas was taking care of Dan and would have changed Dan's IVs and gotten him his broth by this time. I was so thankful for his outstanding help! Caregivers have a tough job! And so do daughters.

Milestone 100 Days

January 3, 2021, Dan hit the +100-day mark from his SCT. 100 days meant he had made it through the most dangerous part. For him, his recovery was behind because of all the problems. At this point, he was on a magnesium IV drip daily, anti-fungal medication, blood sugar checks, insulin injections, steroids because of GVHD, an antibiotic, an immunosuppressant, Pepcid, and a host of other medicines.

Some caused stomach issues. We followed a set course; Penn Home infusion nurse Amanda extracted four vials of blood from Dan's PICC line twice a week, a courier picked up the specimens (called him the blood man), and we waited. One of Dan's Team would call if Dan needed to go to the OPC (Outpatient Clinic) and have some type of infusion. (Red blood for hemoglobin or platelets.) Dan went every two weeks to Philly to see one of the Team.

The second week in January, there was a concern of blood clots forming around his PICC line. Ultrasound showed there were three. Common but sigh, another injection, Lovenox, daily for 12 weeks. He also had swollen feet and legs. The thought was once he was off steroids, which would be sometime in February, he would see a marked decrease in his swelling. The creatine level was still too high, which meant his kidneys were still working too hard. The level was 2.5. It should have been around 1.3. Drink!

Donor Update

The CD3 (T-cells) and CD33/CD66 (Myeloid cells). CD3 83% and CD33/CD66 was 26%. Overall BM 89%. If Dan lost the donor cells or became too low, Dr. Elizabeth would reach out to the donor for more cells. We were praying that did not happen.

Labs Roller Coaster Ride

We were on a roller coaster ride of blood numbers. After his labs were tested at Cherry Hill Penn, the results showed up on mychartpenn about an hour later. It was part of a caregiver's job that I took very seriously. The blood told a story. By understanding how to interpret the complexity of his blood levels, I could be prepared to deal with what was needed next.

The main blood numbers I looked at were red and white blood cell counts, hemoglobin, platelets, glucose, T-cell, HDL, and ANC total. He had little energy if his RBC was below 7, and an infusion was needed. If his platelets dropped to 10, he needed platelets and needed to be less mobile for fear if he got a cut, it would not clot. Is WBC too low? There could be an infection present. As I said, it was a roller coaster, but one that needed to be followed closely.

I saw the labs on mychartpenn before the doctors did. If it was genuinely concerning, I sent a message through mychartpenn, and the whole Team got the message. Lucky them!

I was definitely over the top with my questions. I'm not sure when I realized it, but it hit me one day that I was very impatient. But Dr. Elizabeth assured me it was ok. She wanted me to be a part of the process. But that was a turning point for me; trust and patience go hand in hand. Somewhere during the struggle, I became frantic instead of taking a breath first and thinking. Some of my questions were legit, some, if I had breathed first, would never have been asked. I was becoming a better me.

60th

In November of 2019, Dan turned 60 years old. Our families gave him a Sixties Hippie-themed party, complete with 60's games, music, and groovy dress. Our grandchildren tie-dyed 90 bandanas for each of our guests to wear. It was so much fun! Cait, a family member who is a professional photographer, set up a photo area complete with a Volkswagen bus background; she captured that night perfectly. Dan was upbeat and full of energy. Dan's buddies, new and old, celebrated! We did not know he would be getting an SCT nine months later. Looking back at the pictures filled with memories, Dan's support team was already assembling.

My 60th birthday was July 4th, 2021. Barbara, Dan's mom, was sponsoring a cross-country trip for us, and I had fun planning it! The plan was to drive cross-country from our home state, New Jersey, with stops in Pennsylvania, Ohio, Indiana, Illinois, Iowa, South Dakota, Wyoming, Idaho, Oregon, California, Nevada, Arizona, New Mexico, Texas, Arkansas, Tennessee, Kentucky, West Virginia, and then home. The trip would take a month. I booked unique hotels along the path that took two years in advance to secure.

Dan loves to plan the routes for any of our driving trips. He uses Google Earth and paper maps, which gives him hours of entertainment. He also loves to chat with his boys to get their input. We talked with his Team, and they said, "Dan isn't where he should be, but June is a long way away;" "Making plans is always good for recovery." Tim and Nicholas joined in on the planning since they would be meeting us in Oregon and taking over driving. Tim is great at researching areas for hikes and places to see that are not overrun with tourists. Hidden gems. Nicholas was great on the timing and routes. I did not know what the future held. I did not know if he would be well enough to go, but what I DID know was the doctors were right; looking forward to something, doing something unrelated to cancer, was an excellent uplifter! For both of us.

Work

It wasn't easy to know exactly what to do about work. I thought COVID-19 would have settled by the beginning of the year, and Dan would have recovered so I could leave him home alone a few days a week. Neither of those things happened. The GoFundMe had taken so much of the pressure off, but I wanted to honor those who gave by doing my part in generating funds. So, I had mixed feelings. Should I try? What if I brought a contagion home to Dan or my mom? That was not fair to them.

It wasn't fair to the already overworked co-workers. What

if I had to leave work again? Jen, the director, and Rachael, the supervisor, kept in touch and offered to keep me on and moved me to per diem. That gave me some time!

Perceptions

I knew that his disease was not an easy one to understand. The main problem was that fibrosis causes scarring in the bone marrow. The SCT would kill the cells, but the healthy cells must remove the fibrosis. Dr. Elizabeth shared with us going into the SCT that Myelofibrosis is the hardest SCT because of the fibrosis (scarring). Most times, I think folks just do not get it. Cut it out, shrink it, do more chemo, radiation, and something else. Keeping him safe was difficult, and sometimes I perceived people thought I was going overboard. Folks wanted to visit Dan but were not as cautious as we were. I allowed very few visitors, and those that did see were kept at a distance from Dan. I set up our enclosed porch area where Dan would sit on one side and visitors on the opposite. Mentally it was good for him to see folks. It was hard for his friends and family to see him so sick, but it helped Dan have some normalcy.

Early 2021

I was down for the long-haul, ready to tackle the Goliaths in our path. But I was running out of steam. I could not clean the house each day and wipe everything down. It was becoming exhausting. After his 100-day mark hit (the magical number that Dan was out of the danger zone according to the class.) I changed my routine. I cleaned the bedroom, bathroom, and kitchen every day, but our living space I only cleaned once a week. (Yes, I let those dishes stay in the sink.) I could shop less since Florence, a sweet friend from work, dropped off soups and dinners made by the staff; Stephanie made the best seafood salad for Dan!

After five months of hospital, worry, cleaning, losing my father, and gaining my mother, I needed to breathe. Folks still texted, but they went back to their busy lives. Dan was out of the woods! When it became quieter, I realized how much I was propped up daily by them. But they had lives as well. I missed feeling covered by them. But still, they were never far away from a phone call, text or email.

At day +135, he was getting stronger, and the GVHD seemed to have subsided. Tentatively we were looking toward the future. We continued to work on my 60th Birthday trip, and I allowed myself to get excited! Dan, Tim, and Nicholas finished the driving route, so I booked the remaining hotels. We sent out invites to families across the USA to join us along the route. My sister Kathy and niece Janna would join us in Arizona for my birthday on July 4th. I rented a beautiful Hacienda for a few days at the base of a mountain. My nephew Will and niece Lisa share my birthday and are siblings! I thought it would be awesome if they could meet us, too!

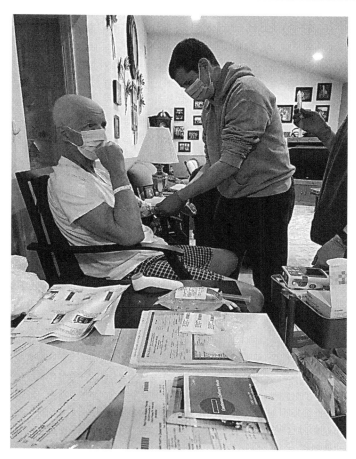

Nicholas Changing Dan's IV Line
Dan's Hair Growing Back

INTO THE STORM

"God never said that the journey would be easy, but he did say that the arrival would be worthwhile."

-Max Lucado-

CHAPTER 13

MIGHT HAVE GOTTEN too relaxed! A week after I sent out family invites via Facebook Events, Dan's shoulders, neck, and back were causing him pain. Infection? Did he pull something? Although still not normal, his bloodwork did not show any real change or cause for alarm. He had a low-grade fever of 99.2. BP and pulse ox were normal. What to do? It was Friday night, February 5th, when it was apparent the pain was more than a pulled muscle. Here we go again! I reached out to the Penn home nurse, and there was no answer. I contacted the other Penn home nurse, also no response. I called the phone number on the outside of our Virtua book in case of emergencies. I was able to talk to a genuinely lovely person who could not help me! I was panicking. I needed someone to tell me what to do! I did not want to decide to take him to the ER. The Virtua nurse said she could not make medical assessments and to contact his doctor. "Take him to the ER for evaluation." That meant a 40-minute drive with Dan, who strongly did not want to go. If I did not hear soon, I would have to decide. I am a calm person normally, but this jarred me. Not now, Lord; he was just beginning to feel there was a chance for healing.

I posted a message on mychartpenn, hoping that the Team monitored it. I continued to take his BP, pulse ox, and temperature every two hours. I knew I would have to go if his fever went over 101.4. I packed him a bag and was prepared. Please, someone call!

Saturday went by, and Dan's fever rose to 100.3, still in the range of keeping him home. I gave him Tramadol for the pain. I sent another message. Sunday arrived, and his fever climbed to 101.1, but his BP and pulse ox were stable.

Sunday evening, a Team doctor called and made it abundantly clear that she did not usually call patients on the weekend and added, "this is a one-time event." Not, "How's Dan?" Not "Let us see if we can figure this out!" Nope! I was surprised; then, I became livid. It takes a lot to make me angry. I will not share my words, but she understood I was furious at her opening response. I am sure my already frazzled emotions did not help either. After we both calmed down, we were able to talk about his symptoms. She spoke with Dan; a plan was created. "No need for ER if fever is under 101.4." "Increase his pain reliever dose to every two hours (I already had), no Tylenol." Tests and an MRI were ordered, I thought for the next day! Nope!

Caregivers again, know your loved one. Dan consistently downplays his symptoms for fear he must go to the ER. You will have to make tough decisions more times than you think.

On Monday, February 8th, he had an MRI scheduled for 10:30 a.m., or so I thought. We arrived at Penn in Philly for the MRI, and there was no parking, so I had to drop off this poor, sick man, in pain, near the front entrance. He walked in, no one helped him, went to Radiology, and it was the wrong day. The appointment was for Tuesday, February 9th. I could not believe my stupidity. By the time he found out, I was able to park in the underground garage, and he came down by elevator and gingerly climbed in. I called to see if they could take him by chance, but they were booked. They were overbooked. Off we went back home. He did not say a word. There was never an angry comment. The next day at 9:00 a.m., we got back in the car, triple-checking the day. I was prepared if they admitted him: clothes, snacks, and drinks. I was able to park, found him a wheelchair, and headed to Radiology for his MRI. While he had the MRI (Magnetic resonance imaging), I messaged the Team to determine if we should wait for the results. I did not receive a message back, so at 12:45, we left for home around noon when he was out of the MRI. He just wanted to get back in bed and sleep. We made a few stops along the way and were home by 1:30 p.m. I hooked up his two IVs and gave him chicken broth, and he fell sound asleep. Around 3:00 p.m. I received a message from his Team: everything was negative; you can go home! Ha-Ha!

Nope

The same day, at 3:35 pm., I missed a call from a Team Doctor saying "Come back now to the ED (Emergency Department); they are expecting him." "Call me!" I reached out to Tim and Nicholas, who were finishing their day at work, to ask if either could drive Dan and me to the ER in Philly, hoping that we could be dropped off out front and I could help Dan get in. Nicholas was home within 15 minutes. Dan was on auto-pilot at this point. He was not communicating at all with me. He was so upset to be going back, and he was trying to stay as calm as possible. The pain was becoming unbearable. I received a message on mychartpenn explaining that Dan has a spine abscess and septic arthritis. During the drive, I talked with a very apologetic Team doctor because it seemed that the radiologist did not give a full report, only a portion. No blame.

As I have mentioned, Penn ER (Emergency Room) was a horrible place to drop anyone off. The new ER was not finished and would be much better. Nicholas had to drop us about 30 feet away from the entrance. I spotted a wheelchair near the entrance door, ran to get it, and met Dan, who sighed with relief.

As we entered the ER, security stopped me. The ER was still under strict COVID-19 protocol. They took Dan and his backpack in and said I could not enter the building. I watched through a window as they wheeled him to the desk. My heart hurt for him and me. I had been taking care of this man, and now when he needed my support, I could not even sit with him. He was alone and feeling poorly. I texted my son and asked him to pick me up, not to park. I got into the car and sobbed. Nicholas put his arm on my shoulder as he drove away, comforting me. How could I leave him? "Lord, please, keep him in your loving hands"! I prayed the rest of the way home.

Another Stay

Answer to prayer! In the ER, Dan only waited two hours to be seen. I spoke to him, and he sounded tired but in good spirits. The right medicine and hydration IV were making a difference. While in the ER, he had another MRI, chest X-ray, and an ultrasound. A bed on Rhodes's 3rd floor opened in the evening. It would be his new home for a bit. I felt better with him being taken care of by the Team. I took a long bubble bath that night!

Caregiver Release Card

So, what does a caregiver do alone without someone to care for? Make a to-do list, of course! Do not try to do your entire list; pick one thing. It snowed, so I cleaned my car off while our exceedingly kind neighbor, Rob, shoveled a path from our door to the car. Now that I would not disturb Dan with noise, I could tackle a few projects. I reorganized the medical supplies and cleaned out the refrigerator. I spent time with mom. I read a historical romance novel. (I know, but they do take me away!) I enjoyed the forced time to decompress and recharge!

Visitation Opened

On Monday, February 15th, six days after he was admitted, visitors were allowed. Just one person and only that one the entire time. When I first saw him, he was sitting in the lounge chair in his room. He looked at me with a bit of a blank expression. I thought he would be excited to see me, but he was not. He just sat there. His emotions were in tatters, like bits of loose material hanging down around him. Although we talked on the phone and he sounded fine, I saw the reality. I quietly sat and waited until he was ready to share what had happened during the last six days.

From the moment he went into ER, the tests began. There were X-rays, ultrasounds, MRIs, a neck bone biopsy, a right arm skin biopsy, elbow joint aspiration, and countless blood tests. Most tests do not bother him, even a closed MRI. But the fourth and final MRI had him in the tube for two hours, then he was removed to add contrast and back in for 30 more minutes. His arms were strapped to his side, and a catcher's mask over his face. The heat was unbearable, and he was unable to move. It altered him. He was able to send his thoughts to another dimension until completed, but it took a toll on him. He has not been the same since. He now struggles with nightmares, anxiety, and moving in and out of reality when he feels stressed. For the first time, he said he experienced a mini break-down. He was not giving up, but he was close. I was not there to be with him, and it hurt. Unfortunately, anxiety was intro-duced to him, and he did not know what to do. I reached out to a counselor, a friend who was able to get Dan past the trauma. We thank our fantastic friend, Doug, for helping Dan get through this challenging episode.

I Took Over

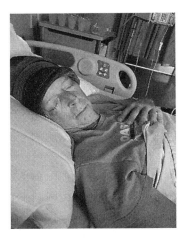

The most crucial aid I gave to Dan was to take over. I took over talking with doctors and nurses, ordered his food, and answered texts and calls. I tried to reassure my family that he just needed time; he would talk to everyone soon. He did not want to think; he did not want to move. Along with making all his decisions for him, I listened and watched to see his needs. I learned from that horrible shower months ago to listen to Dan's spoken and unspoken words. I made mistakes, but I learned.

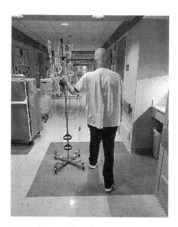

Forgot Masks and Gloves Consistently☺

Although there were times I leaned on emotions, I prayed and checked back in. The doctors prescribed a series of medications to combat the infections. Dan settled, and his condition improved. He was able to connect back in mentally. He would come home with a few more "scars," but he survived. Now it was time to get the home front ready again.

My Triggers

Elise spent the Sunday before Dan came home with me working on another change in his diet. Having a nutritionist in the family is such a gift! She wrote up a plan, and we headed to Whole Foods. Dan's boss, Linwood, and his wife, Deb, dropped off Whole Food gift cards the day before. It was so like God meeting our needs in perfect timing.

In 1992 I was diagnosed with Lyme's Disease. Because the condition was so new, I went undiagnosed for a year. Those little rascal microbes can cause problems. I was treated but left with a few chronic issues. Nothing major unless it is! Bright or flickering lights can cause an episode. Whole Foods store has triggered the response before. After half an hour, I could feel the anxiety starting. I turned to Elise for help. Elise was so sweet and kind, and we checked out quickly. I have learned to live with it, but sometimes it manifests in ways I wish it would not. There is no perfect caregiver. We all have our mountains to climb! After she left for home, I went over my notes and prepared for Dan's homecoming. Then I took a nap!

Donor Update

The CD3 (T-cells) and CD33/CD66 (Myeloid cells). CD3 was 80% and CD33/CD66 was 32%. Overall BM 84%. Downward direction.

HOMECOMING TAKE #4

"It's a funny thing coming home. Nothing changes. Everything looks the same, feels the same, and even smells the same. You realize what has changed, is you."

- Eric Roth-

CHAPTER 14

O N MONDAY, FEBRUARY 22nd, Dan was discharged. The Team determined he'd had a "Perfect Storm." His already weakened state could not manage the loss of steroids, which he had been on for two months since his last hospital stay. It caused his cells (which are not his) to be confused. They were going crazy in areas that did not need them. That is why they could not get a concrete diagnosis. None of his symptoms correlated with another. I will not go into more detail, because you would have to pay me for the biology lesson! And really, I did not understand myself, but he was better. My immediate concern was for him to put on weight, besides wanting the donor cells to play nicely in his sandbox. 135 lbs. was just too low! Unfortunately, he had lost his appetite. The Team did not want to put him on another medication to make him feel hungry. "Wait, and see," the Team said. I asked my family and friends to add this concern to their already lengthy list of prayer requests. I like intentional prayers. Targeted prayers. "For where two or three gathers in my name, there am I with them." Matthew 18:20. Grace.

Care Schedule

Another part of a caregiver's job is to protect the already tired patient. Each time he came home from the hospital, the social worker scheduled several organizations to contact us to go to our home to help, including a home infusion nurse, a care nurse, a physical therapist, and an occupational therapist. One nurse came twice a week to check vitals and draw labs, the other once a week to check vitals and check his overall condition. PT came once a week, and the OT came every two weeks. If scheduled out correctly, we would have eyes on his condition. This was a significant problem the last time he entered the hospital; we did not have enough eyes on him. But too much help can be overwhelming. And, of course, no one was scheduled on weekends!

One of the care teams was adding stress. Every time this person would come, Dan would get annoyed. I cautiously contacted the scheduling coordinator and asked that this person be removed from his care. Now, that was not an easy call, but I also needed to take care of his mental state. The supervisor assured me that it would stay between us. "Some folks just don't click with each other." The stinker was Dan asked me why I did that to the home care person, even though he wanted it done. I was okay with being the "Meany "if it helped him. Life as a caregiver!

Food Changes Again

He was malnourished at 135 lbs. Dan had lost 30 lbs. in 3 months. We needed to start building up the proteins that would aid his recovery. I had all the required foods from my Whole Foods trip. All went well for the first three days; then, his bowels took a turn for the worse. The fat content was too much for his stomach to digest. Over the next few days, I gave him the B.R.A.T. (banana, rice, applesauce, toast) diet, which, unfortunately, along with the bowel issues, brought his weight down to 128 lbs. He also developed a fear of food. Dah! Every time he ate, he hurt.

Bedroom of Comfort

Once his stomach settled, I began the food plan again but limited the fats. Instead of two tablespoons of fats, I added one teaspoon. Unfortunately, fats are high in calories. Limiting them meant he would have to eat more in other food group areas to gain. Nuts were a great source, but he was not hungry. He would drink the broth and eat a few nuts and carbs but little else. I knew nutrition was a huge part of healing.

I contacted the Team to ask if they thought he could begin the medication that would make him hungry. Dronabinol 2.5mg capsules (cannabis without the hallucinogenic) did the trick. He took a dose in the morning, afternoon, and about an hour before dinner. In a week, he went up to 131 lbs. He was craving sweets, so I made him a homemade apple pie using ingredients that would not hurt his stomach. It did not taste the same, but he did not seem to notice. I found "healthy sweets" recipes like muffins, cookies, and pies. My cousin, Chrissy, and her husband Walt are doctors in Nashville, and they sent me some great recipes.

Dan's stomach began to heal, and he felt much better. I was able to add more fats to his diet. He was still so frail. It would take time and patience. I became a short-order cook. Breakfast, lunch, and dinner consisted of all fresh ingredients. I was using a food delivery service; I got what I needed quickly, and there was less exposure to COVID-19. Again, his mother, Barbara, stepped in and helped with the cost. I am forever grateful!

Elise called Dan several times, getting his view on his stomach concerns, and adjusted the food plan as needed. When his stomach did act up, I went back to the B.R.A.T diet, or a combination of the diet but with more proteins. I could see it was going to be a long road. One item I still made every other day was the homemade broth. Elise made our bone broth. The broth would balance the stomach and heal the lining. We both noticed a difference; it helped. I was able to add nutrients to the broth, so if he could only "eat" that at times, I knew he was getting healthy foods.

I went over every meal with him and explained why it was a good fit for his stomach, so his anxiety about eating would lessen. I did this several times, and he relaxed. He began to see hope again. He started back on small workouts that the PT showed him: leg lifts, up and down steps, and working with a cane for balance. I did not want him to lose the calories he could intake. But I knew it was essential to get his muscles working again. It was a balance. He had lost all muscle mass, which was hard on him mentally. I learned when to step in to keep him safe and when I needed to back off. Not easy. Sometimes I felt he could be his own worst enemy. Did I share about the water?

Medication Woes

One of the new medications, over time, caused suicidal thoughts. I found him on the porch, asking me to stay with him or he would harm himself. I knew it was not my husband because he would never harm himself. I contacted the Team, and they ordered a different medication. The doctor was an on-call doctor (because it was the weekend) and said he'd never heard of that medication causing that symptom. I looked it up myself. It was the fourth side effect listed. Sigh. My pharmacy did not have the newly prescribed medication, so I drove 30 minutes away while Nicholas stayed with Dan.

Keeping an eye on side effects was crucial. What is the idiom, the-cure-is-worse- than-the- disease? His loss of memory and foggy brain was a side effect, and he sometimes seemed disoriented. The Team assured us that those concerns should go away as his recovery continued. He was still on medications that usually would have already been removed, but Dan was not a typical case. I added the medication to his "Do Not Take" List.

Using Online Forums

Your doctor is the best source of information. Picking one that meets your needs can be trying but be patient and keep looking. I guess for a long time now, since social media began, "Be Your Own Advocate" has been the mantra. But a word of caution: try not to take this too far and hurt the one you are trying to help.

I joined three groups about Dan's condition. Most people on the forums are just like you; they are desperately researching for answers. Some reveal their ideas through emotions without the aid of scientific studies. Most are not harmful, but some can set your loved one back by trying this or that instead of believing in your doctor.

The social media forums should be thought-provoking, not a cure-all provider. It amazes me how society, through social media, has ventured into the medical field without a degree. God directed us to the Myelofibrosis forum to learn about the Interferon Injections, which gave Dan more time.

The forums can provide hope and comfort. But be wise. I read advice but held it up to the commonsense light. If I found something promising, I would speak to his doctor. Home remedies are essential to healing, but do not let your loved one suffer if they can get faster results through a doctor. Use the forums to connect, but understand everyone is different; case by case, as I stated before, find the doctor who fits you, one who does not tell you what you want to hear but tells you the truth and shows you why. Then put your trust in them and God.

Keeping Him Safe from Himself

Allogeneic (unrelated donor) Stem Cell Transplant +157 days complete. As Dan continued to feel better, he took more chances; working outside without a mask, not protecting the skin on his hands (he developed a few infections on his hands/ arms by bumping into things), working on an old vehicle, (where there was concern about coming in contact with infectious particles) and wanting to help at church (where there was the possibility of COVID-19 exposure).

He wanted to feel normal. There is that word again, normal. He loved helping on the safety team at church. We started with a plan that I would drive him to church and wait in the car near the exit in case he needed to go home quickly for bathroom issues. Nicholas also worked on the safety team and helped Dan when needed. Dan would wear a mask and sit far away from people. He would put on his radio, "20 in the building." In the beginning, he lasted about 30 minutes, then eventually, he made it through the whole service. He would always leave before the congregation left the sanctuary to avoid germs. It was apparent he needed this for healing; he felt needed. His safety team friends were there. He felt the love!

Strange World

Lockdowns closed restaurants and introduced masks. COVID-19 was an extra danger for Dan. It was very contagious, so caution was essential. Dan was not able to be vaccinated. I could not get vaccinated as quickly as the CDC recommended because of my past autoimmune concerns. I had one dose and was just waiting on the doctor's orders for when I could get the second. I leaned into Mathew 6:34, "Therefore do not worry about tomorrow, for tomorrow will worry about itself. Each day has enough trouble of its own." Many of our family members were getting infected. We had a huge scare when Nicholas contracted COVID-19. But through it all, neither Dan nor I got COVID-19.

Up Springs Eternal Hope

March 20th, 2021. Spring. With spring, I have always felt energized. Ready to take on a new season with open arms.

We continued to see Dan's doctor at Penn every two weeks, and the last check-up was encouraging. He asked the doctor if he could start driving. Well, now, that was scary! The doctor said yes if he felt clear-headed. Right!

Driving is a sore subject between Dan and me. To put it mildly, he and I have dramatically different driving styles. While in the car, our "discussions" can get exuberant. One stressful section of highway 295 in NJ loops onto highway

42. After the entrance ramp, it is necessary to cross three busy lanes to head towards the Walt Whitman Bridge to get into Philadelphia. It was never an enjoyable time for us. I asked him once to sit and chill; that did not happen. He is a professional truck driver; I am a country driver with aggressive undertones. I'm glad to say our marriage stays intact! I was NOT ready for him to drive. He drove about five miles for his first experience back behind the wheel. I felt like I was a passenger with a new teenage driver. I was happy when he looked at me and said, "that was enough." Yup, that was enough for ME, although it made me sad that he didn't feel ready. It would just take time. He would gain the confidence again when he got rid of the foggy brain.

Long walks were difficult for Dan. My friend Betty needed the wheelchair returned for her uncle to use because he had contracted COVID-19. I needed to buy a wheelchair. Dan's sister, Dayna, and her husband, Michael, heard about our need and bought Dan a travel wheelchair. Great gift! I can easily lift and take it anywhere. It became our go-to for visits. We no longer had to find and sanitize a wheelchair at Penn's parking garage. It was a significant help to us both!

By mid-April, he weighed142 lbs., a great victory! Again, we had a few spirited (ha-ha) discussions over his intake of liquids. He still did not drink enough, and I saw it on the blood tests. His creatine and urea nitrogen levels were high, indicating he was not drinking enough. Those were the times I got annoyed with him...he had control over this part and could do better. All the doctors and nurses he saw told him the same thing, including the kidney doctor!

Donor Update

The CD3 (T-cells) and CD33/CD66 (Myeloid cells). CD3 was 81% and CD33/CD66 was 83%. Overall BM 82%. "Is it time for more donor cells?" I asked. The Team wanted to give his cells some more time. He had battled back so many times. He had gone through more than most SCT patients. The Team was confident that waiting was all that was needed.

Vaccines

Dan had outpatient visits with different Team members, all connected to his transplant. In the middle of April, he saw Transplant Coordinator Jackie. He was doing well enough to lower the dose or eliminate some medications. He was taking tacrolimus (prevents SCT rejection), Bactrim (prevents bacterial infection), and acyclovir (prevents viruses), along with other medications. And like the other two times, some medication caused side effects. One side effect was trembling hands, making eating hard and self-injections difficult. I told him I would give him the injections, particularly when I was mad at him. Ha-ha. I don't think he saw the amusement in it!

Another side effect was bowel trouble; the medication was tough on the stomach and the balance of minerals. He would get an infusion if his minerals were off, mainly magnesium. Broth helped his stomach, but it wasn't enough. Famotidine (Pepcid) was added to his medications. Generally, by this point, most SCT patients were off tacrolimus, which was the cause of his hand tremors (it also messes with magnesium levels), but with GVHD, they felt it was best to continue.

Jackie removed the PICC line from Dan's arm during one of his two-week visits. No more easy blood draws. The goal after SCT is to have the PICC line removed within six months; any longer than that, and infection and blood clots become a concern. Since Dan already had blood clots form around his PICC line in the past, it was better safe than sorry. After removing it, she sent him to get started on vaccinations at the OPC right there at Perelman.

I was glad he would start getting protected, but I was concerned that the vaccine would kick his immune system too hard and cause his GVHD to return by confusing the donor cells. Vaccines work by building antibodies in the immune system.

I thought he was getting one vaccination. I was extremely surprised, however, when Dan came out of the OPC and told me the nurse had given him three! If I had known her plan, I would have asked her to give him one at a time. He received three for pneumonia, meningitis, and the first round of his DPT (Diphtheria, tetanus, and whooping cough). Within 12 hours, it was apparent the vaccines were working. He didn't feel well, and it caused his stomach issues to come back.

The poor guy could not catch a break! He was back to using Imodium every two hours to get his bowels calmed. The Team noted in his chart to add vaccinations one at a time. There was no proof it was vaccine-related but erring on the side of caution was a good plan.

Unfortunately, GVHD did come back. Again, it made him one sick man—more on that in the next chapter.

Grandbaby #6 (Nolan)

On May 3, 2021, Elise and our son Eric blessed us with our sixth grandchild. Dan had not felt well since his vaccinations. He was battling stomach problems, bowel issues, and fatigue. We were, of course, in constant talks with his Team. Hoping it was one of the medications or lingering vaccines, they lowered the dosage of his medications. I started him back on the

B.R.A.T. diet. I would have gone back to the GVHD 3rd level diet, but I didn't know what was causing the problem.

"Mom, Elise is having the baby!" "Take your time." Yeah, right! I wanted to be as close as I could when he was born. I wanted to celebrate the joy of life.

Since Dan had not been feeling well, I told him I would go up to see the kids (they lived an hour away), stay in a hotel overnight, and come home the next day. (Nicholas was home.) Dan said he "could feel like crap here or there; it didn't matter." He was concerned about the hour drive and his unpredictable bowels, but he said, "I would like to see Eric's family and welcome the new Hurst man." I wanted to sit and cry for him. There were just so many difficulties.

I packed the needed supplies, and we headed out. I wanted to get there before it was dark. We stayed in a hotel room about 10 minutes from where Elise was giving birth. I cleaned the hotel room, including putting on our bed linens and pillows. We stayed one night, and he could see Elise and our newest grandbaby, Nolan, for a few minutes before we left for home. His stomach and bowel issues were getting worse. He tried walking around with the older boys but was not feeling well.

We were now three weeks post-vaccination. I called his Team again and told them, "There must be something else going on." They agreed and sent him to Cherry Hill Penn for lab work and a stool sample.

He had pseudo-C-diff. (Weeks later, doctors said they did not think it was C-diff but another bout of GVHD.) Too many medications and the vaccine side effects overloaded his immune system and caused his stomach lining to say, "Nope!" He was on a powerful antibiotic (vancomycin, he took before with no problem) for two days when he became suicidal. He told me he would go to his workout shed and end it. He implored me, "Don't leave me!" Dan was not thinking clearly. I spoke to the Team once again and stopped the medicine. I filled a new antibiotic at CVS.

He battled Loose stools, nausea, low-grade fever, and fatigue for a few days. They wanted to put him in the hospital, but his mental state from the medication side effect and the visiting hours, although open, were limited. I talked with Dan's primary Team doctor, Dr. Elizabeth, and she agreed he would be better at home. I was getting nutrients and water into him, and the fever was low. I checked his temperature, BP, and pulse ox levels every four hours. It was rough for two days and nights, but he got through. After waiting days for the old medication to expel from his system, I gave him the new medication. This medication seemed to work well. A dear cousin, Lisa, dropped off dinner for Nicholas and me. I was so grateful! She did not know what was happening but got a nudge to bring dinner. What a blessing!

Dan became discouraged. He lost more weight and had to start over in his efforts to gain and move. Over and over, and over, and over. He would get to the point that he saw progress in his healing, and then he would get sick again. Keeping his head in the game and remaining positive was important. He began again. Once again, his friends and family were vital! I always kept in touch with his family through text. His brother, who I mentioned lives in Alaska, came for a visit and spent some time with Dan. That meant a lot to him.

Lance and Samantha

In May of 2021, protocols for COVID-19 became very strict. Only the patient was allowed in the room during doctor's visits. I waited in the atrium on level 2 of Penn, where it was quiet, and we connected via video chat during his visits. While waiting for Dan to call, I received a call from Samantha.

We had met Lance and Samantha during Dan's second hospital stay on Rhodes 7. Lance (an SCT patient) was faithfully walking the halls (I elbowed Dan and teased, "See? That is how it is done!"), and we had a wonderful chat with Samantha. We continued to stay connected through instant messages or phones when life needed a voice.

When she reached out to me that day in May, she said, "Lance is dying. He has GVHD of the liver, lungs, and skin. The Team tried everything, but nothing was working. Donor cells are rejecting and destroying his healthy cells. His organs are shutting down,"

Oh, no! My heart just broke for her and Lance. I knew what they had been through. They fought for the cure, and their fight was ending. "Can you come over?" Samantha asked. "I know it is hard for you and Dan; I understand if you can't.'" There was no pause on my part; of course, I would go over! My next thought was, "How would Dan take this news? Dan was still not healthy and unsure of his outcome.

After my call with Samantha ended, Dan called to say Dr. Elizabeth was there. I reached for my notes to ask questions, but I found it hard to focus. I heard Dr. Elizabeth saying, "Labs show promising signs. The Donor is still fighting. WBC count was low, which is expected because of the recent infection, but they are better." After that call, Dan met me on level 2, and I shared what Samantha told me. True to this amazing man, Dan did not hesitate. "You must go see Samantha," he said. "She wouldn't have asked if she didn't need you." Such a brave, caring man! He had one caveat: "I will stay in the car. I know my limits." Humanity is at its best when you reach down and think of someone else besides yourself and your problems. Isn't that what a trustworthy caregiver is? He had become Samantha's caregiver.

Samantha and Lance rented a row home in Philly, just a

few blocks from Penn. It was a beautiful brick building with early American character, situated on a one-way street. We parked in her driveway. She was waiting at the door. Two wives that understood. We spoke for an hour. I prayed with her for a miracle and shared the peace that only Christ can give. Grief is so unforgiving. It passes by no one. But there is always hope, even when life throws incredible hardships.

It was a difficult visit. Dan and I argued on the way home (while my mom was on the phone, oops!), something about me jumping a curb! We were both on edge and needed to blow off a little steam.

Lance passed away a few days later. So much heartbreak in this life. It was a sharp reality check on Dan's condition. I did not share Lance's passing with Dan for a few weeks. There would be a time when he was better mentally and physically prepared. I needed him to focus on the prize, the cure. When I saw a doctor from Dan and Lance's Team, I told them how sorry I was for their loss. Doctors are humans. Do not forget!

Dan visiting Kitty Hawk, North Carolina
"The airplane stays up because it doesn't have the time to fail!"
Orville Wright

LAUGHTER

There is nothing in this world so irresistibly contagious as laughter and good humor."

-Charles Dickens-

CHAPTER 15

NEVER UNDERESTIMATE THE power of laughter. Caring for your loved one is not just a physical exercise. I reached out to his friend Jimmy several times to connect with Dan. If you can take your loved one away for a little while, it will aid healing. During his low times, the change was remarkable. When Dan was down, I would reach out to Jimmy and humorous friends and family. "If you get a chance, he could please use some laughter." It helped keep Dan's spirits up and let him forget his struggles for a little while. They would tell the story even if Dan did not seem interested. After a time, Dan could not help but become immersed. Laughter is so good for all of us. I could always tell who Dan was talking to by his tone. He was able to step away from his troubles and think about something else. It was helpful mental healing.

By June 1st, Dan's condition had improved. He had gained a few more pounds and was up to 145 lbs.; his head was clearer, and he was driving like a pro (his words). He still had residuals of GVHD rash on his back and infection in his eyes, but it was all clearing up. His hard work doing PT had begun to develop noticeable muscle. His WBC was in the normal range, and his RBC count was too low, but the numbers were steady. Unfortunately, he was considered chronic GVHD, and it would be a matter of time before it emerged.

GVHD was a leading factor of morbidity in Allogeneic (unrelated donor) Stem Cell Transplant patients, at approximately a 50% mortality rate. (cancernetwork.com) Much has been done via study trials to combat GVHD within the past few years. As I shared, Dan was in a study during his hospital stay in November 2020.

Study Coordinator Kim met us in the atrium on our way to Dan's June visit at Penn. (Fun fact, we almost got stuck in an elevator, my nerves were a wee bit shot!) There was a new trial that she thought fit Dan perfectly. The hope was that the medication would help control or reverse his chronic GVHD condition. To be honest, I was a bit deflated. We were supposed to leave on our amazing cross-country trip in three weeks. If he joined the clinical trial, he would need to be monitored weekly for a month. UGH! Do not get me wrong; there was no doubt what we were going to do, but, UGH! I had hoped we would get away without any further complications. But we had not come all this way to fail or lose what could be a lifesaving treatment. He had never had a string of more than six consecutive weeks that he felt good since his SCT. What would happen if we were in California, and he became ill? Of course, we would join the trial. We would go on our trip another time. I would be 60 for a year!

We consulted with Dan's Team, and they were not excited about him going so far away. Dr. Elizabeth said, "His GVHD is still fragile. Dan has survived what many do not, and he is getting stronger, but if it works, this clinical trial will help his survival rate in the future." Lance passed away from GVHD complications. The doctors were invested in Dan, clinically and emotionally. We trusted them.

Dan and I encouraged Tim and Nicholas to continue with the trip. Part of the trip was not refundable (including their airfare), and we wanted them to be able to enjoy it. They had an exciting time and recorded special memories. It's funny; I was not envious; it just felt right—all in God's timing.

Another God send during this time appeared when my work staff at the assistant living facility began making and dropping off food every Thursday. They would send me their weekly menu, and I picked foods that best worked with Dan's healing. Florence, a dear friend, brought us the meals. The most helpful offering was their soups. They brought me homemade broth soups: such a blessing and a time-saver. I will never forget the generosity of the dining room staff and the kitchen staff!

Clinical Trial #2
Investigational Drug Itacitinib, INCB039110, IRB834433
400 mg tablet

Dan had to meet two criteria: chronic GVHD and mild GVHD in two body areas. He met both. Chronic meant he had had GVHD more than three times since his SCT. The trial drug was supposed to lower the chance of GVHD coming back in the future. Of course, it was a trial, but results seemed positive in other patients. During the first few weeks, his RBC and platelets dropped, which would have been a concern, except other patients in the study had the same result and later leveled. He was taking four pills per day. Each pill was 100 mg. Labs were done weekly and noted in the study. Dan gave 18 vials of blood at the four-week mark of the study. The next study labs were required in two-week increments. Pulmonology function tests were performed every four weeks, to gauge his lung capacity. His energy level dipped in the first few weeks, but once his body adjusted to the medication, we began to see positive results. The rash on his back and redness in his eyes went away.

On July 12th, the last of our monthly two-week visits, Elizabeth (MD), Linda (PA), and Kim (CN) came smiling into the private clinical trial room where we were waiting. (This is a space where the in-room doctor would come in to speak to guests or patients and have trial procedures.) This was promising. "After reading his current lab tests today, we won't need to see you for a month." They gave us the green light to go on our trip!! "Have a fun time but stay safe." "We will need labs in about two weeks." We headed to the parking garage like two little kids, with extraordinary joy! We would not have to see the doctor for four weeks! Imagine that! We talked on the way home to ensure this was the best course of action. He and I just wanted to get away from cancer for a while. Our budget was going to be very tight, so we changed some of the "To-Dos" on the birthday wish list. Nicholas came home just as we were heading out and took a picture of us driving away. We were on an adventure! Thank you, Barbara, for sponsoring our trip! Thank you, Lord, for your healing grace!

Donor Update

The CD3 (T-cells) and CD33/CD66 (Myeloid cells). CD3 was 100% and CD33/CD66 was 100%. Overall BM 100%. Praise the Lord! He was finally fully grafted! (Engraftment means your new cells are working properly and starting to rebuild your immune system.) The Team was right. "Let's wait and see."

The Celebratory Road Trip

Keeping him safe was necessary, so cleaning supplies and our bedding made the trip. We also took his electric bike so he could enjoy "hiking" with me. During hotel stays, I sprayed furniture with fabric cleaner, cleaned toilets, wiped sinks, wiped door knobs, etc. We broke our driving up (except the first two days) to no more than five hours each day. I love to drive and have no problem with city driving. Dan drove in the morning when his energy was highest, and I drove in the afternoon. When we left New Jersey, Dan struggled with the fear of being far away from his Team of doctors, but by the time we reached Chicago, he was fine, and the trip became healing for his mind.

We stayed at my brother & sister-in-law's house (Ernie & Barb) in Iowa and my sister Kathy's in Texas, where we got to see lots of extended family. We visited with nieces and nephews along the path. We accepted the hospitality of friends Ed and Roxanne in Houston, Texas, and made a quick Nashville stop with my cousin Chrissy and her family. Seeing friends and family made the trip incredibly special. All of them have prayed and supported us through this long journey.

Death Valley Time Capsule
Tim:2021, Dan:1985, Nicholas:2021

The Redwood Forest topped my list of unique places. I had a few meltdowns with the cliffs in many states; who knew I was afraid of heights? But we made it through. We stopped at a LabCorp in Nevada to have Dan's blood drawn for Penn. He was feeling well and had put on more weight.

We exchanged our 35th-anniversary wedding rings (I'm glad we waited!) in the Grand Canyon. (His was silicone; we bought mine in the Grand Canyon gift shop). It was an extraordinary moment. A tourist offered to take our picture. It is a memory I will always cherish. On August 2, we arrived home, just two days before his next visit with Penn. We loved our trip and would do it again! We have always loved being together. We drive with no music and just chat or sit in comfortable silence. I would play soft piano music when he slept. We drove approximately 8,000 miles. The trip was cathartic and majestic, and I know I left more hotel rooms cleaner than they were when we got there! (Where is my tip?)

He saw his Team on August 4th. His blood numbers had continued to improve, and he was feeling great. They lowered the clinical trial dose to 300 mg. The rest of August was uneventful with his condition, and I started to relax the intensity of the house cleaning. Honestly, I was tired of cleaning, period!

Fresh Air

Dan's cousin Joe and his wife Barbara own a house at the Jersey shore. For recovery healing, they offered the place to us for four days, from Monday, August 23 until Thursday, August 26. It was such a blessing! Joe met us at the house and helped me carry in our food and luggage. Dan is a major fan of Joe; he has his own physical concerns but reaches out to Dan often to see how he is.

The weather was in the mid-'90s, so our plan was early morning or late evening walks and swimming. A few of the medications called for complete coverage from the sun. A trapper hat (a hat with flaps) covered perfectly. On the first day, we just hung out and enjoyed the bay view from the porch. Dan loves watching birds; we saw egrets, terns, and oystercatchers. Once the sun went down, the Fowler frogs became a noisy choir. We walked about ¼ mile on the boardwalk and strolled the beach on the second day. The electric bike stayed at the unit.

Dan seemed "off" on Wednesday. He was wrapped up in a

blanket, while I was in shorts and a tank top. He also did not eat much. I knew the signs; he was getting sick again. He began running a slight fever, and his BP was going up. His stomach seemed okay, but we knew it was best to go home. I packed the car Wednesday after dinner, and we left early Thursday morning. I sent a message to the Team.

Tides are Turning

His Team wanted to wait and see. His body was producing enough T-cells (cells inside WBC that help fight infection). By Saturday, August 28th, his stomach and bowels, were getting worse, and he was running a low-grade fever, 99.02. Sunday, his fever was 100.0. On Monday, it was 101.5. His Team said to bring him into the OPC at Penn for evaluation. They did bloodwork and gave him an IV for dehydration. The OPC nurse sent him home since his bloodwork looked good, and he felt better after a saline IV to help with dehydration.

Although happy to be going home, I knew he had an infection. We were back over the next day when his fever spiked to 103. He did not want to go! "I don't understand; why is this happening again?" he asked. He had been doing so well! He looked at me with tears in his eyes. I did not know what to tell him, but I knew he needed to return to Penn. I physically helped him out of bed and helped him to get dressed. He was so exhausted. I called and told the Team when we arrived. "Wait in the car; we will send someone to get him to radiology for a chest X-ray." (They needed to follow COVID-19 protocol because of his fever.)

An assistant from the radiology department met us in the parking garage and wheeled Dan to a private room. As we waited for a chest X-ray, I held him and prayed. He fell asleep on my shoulder. After the X-ray, he began to shake even though he was wrapped in two layers of blankets and both of our hoodies.

After the chest X-ray, I wheeled him to the fourth floor into another private room to see Dr. Elizabeth, and the Study Coordinator, Kim. Dr. Elizabeth asked us questions, trying to figure out the cause of the infection. The X-ray was clear; there was no pneumonia. I shared what we had done in the last few weeks. I asked if it could be a side effect from the clinical trial. "Remember the first clinical trial drug?" I stated, "Dan had a bad reaction." We were shocked when she indicated that the first clinical trial saved his life. Even though it was only one dose, only about 10% would have survived what he had last November. The drug reversed the dying of his cells that were so precious and new. Wow! God's special protection once again. But it was evident to everyone in the room except Dan that he could not go home.

"I know you don't want to go, Dan, but you must be admitted to the hospital." I could tell it was hard for her to give Dan the news. He was devastated. "I do not think I can sit in the ER for five hours again! It is too hard," he spoke.

She sent him to an infusion room on the third floor for an IV to help with dehydration while she secured him a bed in the hospital. He would not have to go through the ER. (Later, this was pivotal to his outcome.) The infusion nurse gave him a high dose of Tylenol, which worked for about two hours to control the shaking and fever. He was having BP problems as well. I held him, gave him a snack, and made him drink as best I could. He slept on and off in the bed, but it was never a quiet sleep. I brought a book and read the first page for an hour.

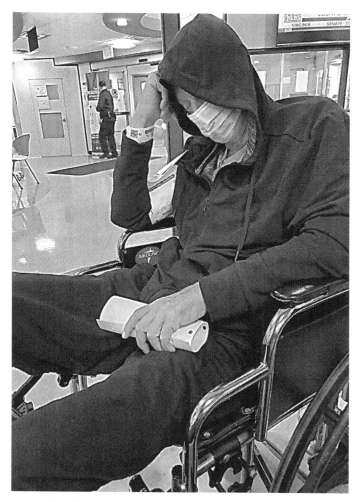

The Hospital at the University of Pennsylvania

FAITH

"Faith is unseen but felt, faith is strength when we feel we have none, faith is hope when all seems lost."

-Catherine Pulsifer-

CHAPTER 16

Tuesday, August 31st. Reliving this day, this moment in time is extremely hard for me. I want to share; I want you to know that you can get through anything, even when you cannot see a way. God will always walk with you, carry you! But reliving through sharing is difficult.

At 5:00 p.m., we went to the admittance department in the hospital. Before we left, the OPC nurse gave Dan another high dose of Tylenol. We filled out office paperwork and waited for his hospital room to be ready. We sat in a room alone with a TV and chairs. Dan kept falling asleep but could not get comfortable. I began noticing around 6 p.m. that his fever was increasing. His eyes and cheeks were flaming red. Unfortunately, another hour passed; the high dose of Tylenol would not last much longer. The shaking started, and I held him. "Please Lord, he needs help, Please Lord!" How much longer? Ten minutes later, the admittance person told us to go up to Rhodes's 3rd floor; the room was ready. It was 7:15 p.m. I began wheeling him to Rhodes 3, and on the way, his shaking became so uncontrollable he barely stayed in the chair. He had his head down, a hoodie covering his head, blankets and coats tucked around his body. I was pushing him while holding him in the chair. He could not keep himself upright. A doctor stopped me in the hallway leading to the Rhodes elevators. "Is he okay? Can I help?" I thanked him and never paused; I prayed I was getting Dan the help he needed. I had no time to stop and explain.

As I entered Rhodes's 3rd floor, a nurse at the other end of the hall took one look and came running while calling others to help. Three nurses, the floor manager, and a coordinator began the work he needed. Lifting him to the bed took all of us because of his shaking. His heart was in A-fib. He was shaking so hard they could not hold him on the bed. "What year is it?" "Who is the President of the United States?" "What is your name?" No answer, just a blank look.

His blood pressure was dangerously high, and his fever was now 104.2. I helped take his clothes off and stood back. During this coordinated chaos, I was called out to the hallway and asked about his medical directives. "Will he agree to a ventilator if needed?" "Are we to resuscitate him?" I was glad I knew all the answers. Caregivers, this is HUGE! You need to be ready to speak for those who do not have a voice. The extra added stress is removed if you already know your loved one's wishes.

What had happened? He was great four days ago. The charge nurse gave him an injection to stop the shaking. The defibrillator (used to get his heart regulated) was ready if needed. Intravenous medication, cold packs, another injection; I do not know what they did, but they tried to save his life.

I texted our families to pray. I needed to reach out, to have them know that we needed a miracle. Dan needed those prayer warriors! I did not reach out to Dan's mom; I thought it best to let Dayna, who lives close by, keep her posted.

Dan's sister Dayna, brother Dave, and our kids jumped on texting and kept me sane. "It will be ok; we are praying, mom." "Dan's strong; he will get through this, Sue; look at all he has already accomplished." I prayed! At times, caregiving is too hard, and the moment's loneliness becomes overwhelming.

God gave me/us supporters, and I will never forget, and they will never understand what they did for me that evening! I had never experienced up close the hecticness of losing a life. My endorsement of nurses grew that day!

After 45 minutes, the nurses had Dan stabilized, and he was in a restless sleep. "The next few hours would be crucial," the Charge nurse said. His temperature was slowly coming down. I looked at the clock; it was 8:15 p.m. One hour. It seemed like a lifetime. A nurse checked on his vitals every 15 minutes for two hours. He stayed stable! Would it have been too late if I had stopped and received help from the doctor in the hallway to Rhodes? By 10:00 p.m., his breathing became even; his sleep was calm. Thanks to those amazing God-gifted staff, and the home prayer warriors, he had pulled through. I sent out the last text; "stable, thank you. I will keep you posted." That was at 10:15 p.m.

Around 11:00 p.m., he woke and asked why he was naked. (His sister said I blew a perfect opportunity; she always adds levity.) "What happened"? he asked. I did not share what had just happened. I told him he had such a high fever that he could not remember, which was true. There would be time to share when he felt better this night, and I could tell him without tearing up. I left around midnight. All would be well.

With solid antibiotics, he showed marked improvement over the next few days. They never found out the cause of the infection, which became sepsis. (Sepsis syndrome results from a generalized inflammatory and procoagulant response to infection). They believe it started in the lining of his stomach, which caused his digestive bacteria to be absorbed into his stomach lining and damaged the lining, which allowed bacteria to enter the bloodstream. The sepsis syndrome in immune-compromised patients causes organ failure. He was a miracle! The same mantra we have heard from the beginning: "Dan's body does not act like a normal Stem Cell Transplant patient." Thank you, Lord!

He remained in the hospital for seven days. I know two caregivers stayed with Dan so I could get rest, but I cannot remember who. He was coming home! On my "resting" days, I did my usual: cleaned, prepared food, and picked up prescriptions from the pharmacy. I visited my mom at her house and told her what had happened. She already knew because I asked Nikki to call and tell her after I knew Dan would be okay. She cried. I kept the story simple and did not share everything. Dayna and her son, Jake, waited until Dan was stable before sharing what had happened with Dan's mom, Barbara.

HOMECOMING TAKE #5

"Although the world is full of suffering,
it is also full of the overcoming of it."

-Helen Keller-

CHAPTER 17

ON SEPTEMBER 7TH, Pharmacy again came to Dan's room with instructions. The charge nurse gave us an after-visit summary and set up Dan's follow-up appointments. The ride home was quiet. I wish I knew what he was thinking, or maybe not! I knew he was different since he complimented me on my driving. "You're a great city driver," he said. Now I was worried! Ha-Ha!

Steroids made him hungry, and he wanted to stop at Outback Steakhouse. This man wanted a steak, so he got a steak. He ate everything, along with a potato! We had the whole place to ourselves! We were very cautious, and of course, I wiped down his seating area.

He would be eating GVHD 3rd level diet to add weight and protect his stomach lining. This was a low fiber, high protein diet. His nutritionist, Ryan, had recommended going slow in the hospital, but Dan did not have many restrictions unless his stomach told him otherwise. I pulled out my notes and slowly worked up to a regular diet each day. Just six weeks ago, we were far away. Thank you, Lord, for keeping him safe on the trip!

+365 Days Celebration

On September 25th, 2021, Dan hit the one-year mark! As you have read, it was a rough year! Every time he started making significant progress, something would happen. He never gave up! Pride is too small of a word for what I felt for this amazing man! We celebrated him and were thankful. Since he was just in the hospital, I kept the celebration small at the house but reached out to everyone on our "Prayers for Dan" Facebook page and asked them to text, call or send a card on that special day.

A caregiver shares times of triumph! Do not always share the negative with your supporters. Be positive. Reminding folks of this impressive man's progress was a reward I will always cherish! God has indeed blessed!

What We Have Waited to Hear

On Wednesday, October 27, 2021, Dan had a Bone Marrow Biopsy. His first biopsy was in 2016 in an operating room with sedation; all subsequent procedures were in the office or his hospital bed, usually performed by a nurse practitioner or doctor. He would lie on his stomach on the exam table and be given a local anesthetic. The inserted needle would aspirate the marrow. (Dan said again that it was a weird feeling of pain inside his body. He said it gave him the heebee jeebees!) The procedure took about 30 minutes. He was sore and tired for almost a day. The biopsy had been performed four times since June 2020.

On Tuesday, November 9th, 2021, I received a phone call from Dr. Elizabeth. She said, "I could not wait to tell you both that Dan's cancer is gone!" Oh, my! Dan was outside filling up his bird feeder. I ran out. "Dan, this phone call is for you," I said. He paused, took the phone, and his entire world changed. In the middle of our yard, we both shed happy tears and praised the Lord. "The immature cells are gone; the fibrosis is reversed," continued Dr. Elizabeth. Five minutes later, Dr. Linda called and shared the exact news! "I could not wait to tell you!" she spoke.

All he had been through, all those struggles. I asked him if he would do it again, knowing what he knew now, what he would be facing. He took a deep breath and said, "Yes." The alternative was dying. He fought for a cure and was getting his life back. After he and I told our mothers, we got on texts and the "Prayers for Dan" Facebook page to share the miracle of Dan's healing. Dad, if you can hear me, you were right; Dan will be okay!

Last Thanksgiving, my mom and I sat at a table with all the fixings and no appetite. We (Nicholas, Dan, Rachel and I) decided to have a small Thanksgiving dinner at our house for nine people. Nicholas brought down his Cape Cod red dish set, and I began preparing the home and the menu. I was so excited!

Saturday, November 20th, Dan began with another low fever. The fever hovered around 100.0 all weekend. I took his BP and pulse ox every 4 hours, and both looked steady. Because of the sepsis in September, the Team wanted to see him. On Monday, the 22nd, he was headed to Penn for an evaluation. His fever went to 101.2. They did not send him home; he went to the ER and was admitted to the hospital. This was Penn's new hospital that had only been open for a few months. Diagnosed with pseudo-C-diff with a UTI (urinary tract infection) caused again by medicines. Medications that suppress the immune system can increase the risk of infections. The Team decided to put him on an antibiotic but not as strong as C-diff would be called for. I called our guests and canceled Thanksgiving at our house. We knew we had to be very cautious every time he came home.

He was on the 12th floor of the new Hospital of the University of Pennsylvania. It was a genuinely nice room with a view of Franklin Field. He did not need to be in the hospital for long. The doctors said they wanted to make sure what happened in September did not happen again. His fever stayed under 101, and his vitals were stable. He celebrated his 63rd birthday, the second in hospital. He received a package from the Headstrong Foundation. It is an amazing organization that gives all oncology patients a treat bag. Inside were sweet cards made by kids.

THE PROMISE OF A NEW BEGINNING

"For I know the plans I have for you,' declares the Lord, 'plans to prosper you and not to harm you, plans to give you a hope and a future."

-Jeremiah 29:11-

Special Tribute

Thank you to the fantastic Team at Penn University, Abramson Cancer Center in Philadelphia. Dr. Elizabeth, Dr. Mary Ellen, Linda PA, Kim CRN, Jackie CRNP, Ryan CN, Dr. Joseph, Tatiana NP, Aly RN, and the many other Team members and staff who dedicated their lives to helping others. We are truly blessed! Thank you to Dr. Rachel in Mount Holly NJ, Dr. Genovese, Dan's original Primary, and Dr. Walker for setting us on the path to the cure.

CHAPTER 18

E CAME HOME on Thanksgiving Day. Nicholas and Rachel celebrated with us, and we enjoyed our time. Unlike homecomings from other hospital stays, he felt good. The two infections were caught early, and his body was able to jump in and help the healing process along with antibiotics. Although it was another hospitalization, we knew he had turned a corner. His body was healing from within. Hope has grown stronger!

I left my employment in November, and I will miss the staff. They did not need to, but they stuck by me. I am incredibly grateful. In December, Dan's health insurance costs increased to an amount we could not pay. After researching, I found a great insurance broker, Kathie, who helped us sort through the tangle of insurance. She was familiar with Penn and went the extra mile to ensure Dan had coverage for his continued recovery and a policy we could afford. I selected a different policy for myself, which was more cost-effective.

Each year I give gifts following a theme at Christmas. In 2020, I crafted homemade crocheted items… I sound like a granny indeed! (It was the first time in 20 years I picked up crochet needles.) I have sweet memories of sitting by Dan's bedside, working on someone's gift, which gave me comfort, or sitting with my mom in the living room as I worked. The gifts were a bit wonky, but love was in each stitch.

In 2021, I made homemade treats and meals. There were

cakes, muffins, gingerbread cookies, fruit bars, peanut butter bars, three types of bread, pot pies, and stuffed shells. Unfortunately, some folks did not get their meals because my freezer was not working, so I had to toss four of each. I ran out of time to make more, but I gave everyone a lovely basket. Grandbabies, of course, got something to open! Not having the funds to spend was strange, but it was fun being creative. Besides, Christmas is not about the gifts, except one, that beautiful baby in the manger!

Dan will remain on the clinical trial for a while, showing marked improvement with his chronic GVHD. He is enjoying his newfound freedom from his ever-watchful caregiver. (Letting go of the invisible leash, as one of his buddies said.) Dan helps with household chores; I asked the doctor to add emptying the dishwasher to his after-visit summary, which she did! We chuckle when we think of it (at least I do). Finding my way back to being a wife and not his caregiver is difficult. I understand the phrase "new normal."

My mom is living in her house full-time. Family and friends call and visit often. Mom's sister, Christine, lost her husband and a daughter in 2019; they lean on each other for healing. The most challenging time in any grief is when things settle, and the calls, cards, and visits stop. My mom loves the Lord and rests in Him daily as she listens to her books and learns to navigate a new life. I am so glad my parents brought me to church so I would know the hope.

My father-in-law Bill is slowly losing himself to the unforgiving disease of vascular dementia. Seeing such a great man get lost in his world is hard. Family and friends often help, but as most caregiving, it rests primarily with one person.

Barbara and Dan still talk most nights around 7:15 p.m. I think that will always be their time. He gets daily morning texts from his sister, Dayna, and his mom. "Day +402," "Day

+403," "Day +404." Never underestimate the power of family love!

Remembrance

Several patients who began their SCT journey around the same time as Dan are no longer with us. Lance's journey ended in May 2021. I often think of his wife, Samantha, without her husband, and their adult kids without their dad.

Pastor Dave from an online group, "Voices of MPN," lost his battle in September 2021. He never faltered in lifting someone or helping in any way he could! We lost sweet Pearl (the name given by MPN Group), who was an encourager to all. Her daughter said Pearl always thought of others with this horrible disease and prayed daily for them. And there were many more.

Cancer is cruel. I do not know why God allowed Dan to survive and not others. Isaiah 55:8-11 says, "For my thoughts are not your thoughts, neither are your ways my ways," declares the LORD. "As the heavens are higher than the earth, so are my ways higher than your ways and my thoughts than your thoughts."

Future Promise

In February 2022, we drove to Louisiana to visit Eric and Elise and their mission team from Reach Global. The team's outreach is to help those who cannot afford cleanup and repairs to their homes after disasters and to bring hope. They pray with every homeowner and share Christ's love.

Hurricane Ida's destruction in the summer of 2021 will keep the teams busy. Dan had limited energy but was able to join the clean-up effort. I helped with administration duties and spent cherished time with Elise and the grandbabies. Dan was encouraged by how far his strength and stamina had grown. He was back to his workout schedule. He wants to be a productive part of society and work. The company Dan worked at for 33 years was sold to another concrete business. He investigated working for them, but the hours were too long. He knew his limits.

In March 2022, Dan helped Tim and Erin with outside cleanup, continuing to build his strength while looking for work. He was getting stronger each week; he was ready. The doctors okayed him to work if he took precautions. He eventually found a job in his industry, Artistic Materials Inc. He gets tired but is so happy to be back!

One stem cell transplant, one donor, six hospital stays, and a $ figure of almost three million (thank you, insurance, and GoFundMe), and he is ready to begin life again. He kept his eye on the prize!

Working with Global Reach Team 2022
Weight 165lbs

His new boss gives him time for his monthly appointments and is understanding of his condition. What a blessing!

Years of Learning and Growing

2015 began my most significant learning and growing experience. If I learned but did not grow, what was the purpose? Some moments will remain private, but most I have shared. I found I could do so much more than I thought, but I reached out for help when I could not. Reaching out is something I have never been comfortable with, especially as an introvert.

I was angry, frustrated, and confused at times. I did not know the right questions to ask. I felt like a lifeguard that could not swim! I realized that my feelings came from fear and the need to control. I let that go. I thought it would make me weak, but it made me strong! Tomorrow always came.

Instead of a fevered request, my faith has settled into a quiet knowledge. There is not anything I could ask that God does not know or for which He already has plans. A beautiful connection between father and daughter. I ask; he knows. In my humanity, I would like to think that my earthly dad is talking to my heavenly dad and saying, "everyone needs a Susie in their life." I hope I made them proud.

I learned to be patient with myself, doctors, family, and friends and listen until I have ALL the facts. I learned to forgive myself for making wrong decisions; I am not perfect until I see Jesus. I learned to take direction from others and that doctors are human and do their best. I learned a quietness that allows me to see life calmly and a knowledge that, yes, tomorrow would take care of itself. Life seems more straightforward and filled with greater joy!

I tear up when I think of the amazing, giving folks that supported us. Family, friends, neighbors, and co-workers stayed connected, made us laugh, and lifted us when we needed it the most. I wish I could name them all. Several are going through their health battles. I found kindness in doctors, nurses, cleaning crews, parking attendants, security guards, etc. The character of the heart is found in small areas that mean much and cost little. Most will never know the lifeline they left for us to grab when we needed it the most, and an example followed.

The relationship between Dan and me has grown into a deeper bond. "I married you for life and not for lunch!" (I heard that from my mother-in-law.) Dan and I have always been opposites. In the '90s, we took the Meyers-Briggs Personality test with our church (which showed our innate personality gifts). Out of married participants, we had the most extreme personality differences. "You two could not be more opposite if you tried." "How do you make your marriage work?" Dan and I always agreed on two crucial parts of our marriage: a relationship with Jesus Christ and finances. There are phases in relationships: early marriage with children, middle age, and retirement. Each step brings changes and new challenges. Sickness is a dynamic that can strengthen or damage. I did not have my husband for two years; I had a patient. He did not have a wife; he had a caregiver. We are finding our way back and developing a new husband/wife dynamic; we are grateful, stronger, and loving.

My respect and love for my husband have grown. He never gave up through a series of needles, tests, nausea, constant stomach issues, medication woes, and much more! He told me he would never look back once he decided to fight and leave it in the Lord's hands. As I write, I remember the horrible struggles he went through, and I am tearing up. Kindness was always his mantra. He never spoke a mean word to me or anyone else. I learned by watching him. Would I be like that through a struggle? I hope my measure is never taken. I am so enormously proud of him! I am glad God brought us together to do this thing called life…now I need a nap!

My brother Rick and Sister-in-law Nikki call Dan the Superman! He sure is!

<u>Superman</u>
<u>Man of Steel</u>

Faster than a speeding bullet, more powerful than a locomotive, able to leap tall buildings in a single bound. The infant of Krypton is now the Man of Steel: Superman!

~RELUCTANT EXTROVERT~

Your journey will be unique. My advice is to talk with God often. Find support folks who will not add extra stress but quietly be there. Do not lose your humanity while taking care of your loved one. Do not be afraid to share your needs with others. Keep a logbook. Be prepared to experience a journey you will never forget and share it with others. Your story, your experience, will help others through their journeys. Watching a loved one suffer is not fair, but you are their gift. Be the best you can be in that moment, and let God help you serve your loved one. A caregiver gives up the life they know to help those they love. It is not easy to be out of a comfort zone. I found that, after the dust settled, it was rewarding. Most will not understand what you will go through. Be easy on them. This is your journey to take. Theirs will be in another form. Step away and breathe when you find yourself slipping into fear or doubt. Not far because your gift, your calling, is needed. You have been given a great privilege, cherish it and cherish the loved one in your care.

And if your loved one's journey ends sooner than hoped, know that this is just a temporary stop, this place we call earth. Our heavenly home has no more pain, no more sorrow, and our loved ones will be waiting to welcome them into their cherished home. As for this reluctant extrovert, I plan on living life with a newfound me!

*"Come to me, all you who are weary and bur-
dened, and I will give you rest."*

Matthew 11:28

Dan on Mackinac Island 2019

BONUS EDITION

HOSPITAL CAREGIVERS

Dan's hospital caregivers wanted to share their perspectives with you. Dan, the good-natured fellow who allowed me to write this book to encourage you, has also added his thoughts.

His Mother– Barbara

When I learned, in June of 2020, that my son, Dan, had terminal cancer with possibly less than a year to live, my first thought was denial – my mind refused to accept what he was telling me. It just was not possible for one of my children to die before I did.

My second thought, after he told me the only "cure" for Myelofibrosis (a/k/a Bone Marrow Cancer) is Stem Cell Transplant (SCT) was, "Oh, thank heaven – there is a way to fix this!"

Fortunately for him – and me – he was thinking the same thing.

I worried then because they said the chances of success for SCT is 63% to 70% for someone his age (62). That alarmed me until my other son, David, told me that 18 years ago when his wife, Nancy, was diagnosed with Stage 3 breast cancer, her percentage was less than 60%. She is presently still cancer-free and quite healthy.

Daughter-in-law, Susie, became a Professional Caregiver, in every sense of the word. There is no way I can repay her for the wonderful, lifesaving care she has given my son over the past two years.

Of course, all of us offered to jump in and "take care" of Dan during his long stay in the hospital. I was at home doing a different kind of "caregiving" for my dear husband, who is in the later stages of Alzheimer's. But family members managed to step in for me so I could spend some days with my Dan and give Susie a rest. So, I stepped into a world of rubber gloves and gowns and masks and getting to know some wonderful people who cared for Danny day and night. During those days we chatted, I read while he slept, I walked with him when he could – pushing his IV pole as we walked. I watched him play with his food and wished I had a kitchen in the hospital so I could fix him his favorites and give them to him hot! And I prayed a lot.

We live an hour from Dan and Sue and driving back and forth is saved for special times – it is difficult for me and at that point impossible for him. So, I would call at 7:15 every night to check on his day and talk to him about mine. At Christmas I bought the Echo device for all of us, so we could see each other while we chatted. Sometimes we had so little to talk about we would discuss our menu for the day! But our daily contact helped me as much as I hope it helped him.

He is still dealing with some GVHD pop-ups, but he is dealing with them from a position of strength. I love to hear him planning trips, interacting with his grandchildren, being thoughtful and kind to his Dad, and enjoying life. I still text him a "Good Morning" every day and he still answers me. And we still chat frequently at 7:15.

When I realize where Danny is in his life now, and the future he now has, I thank God again for the doctors and their skill at U of P, Susie, and my family. And for Danny's "I can do this" attitude. We all agreed:

He could … and he did.

His Sister– Dayna

I honestly can't remember the day I found out that my big brother had cancer. I do recall, however, that my reaction to this diagnosis was a firm, "Nope."

Dan is four years older than me. My oldest brother, Dave, and I inherited the dark hair/dark eyes from our mom. Dan was the blond, blue-eyed, perfect kid. In fact, he called himself "perfect."

It was around the time that our dad was diagnosed with vascular dementia that I first learned about Myelofibrosis, a word that now autocorrects on my cell phone. I went into denial. My big brother could absolutely not have cancer. He was the perfect kid.

I felt helpless. In 2020, in the midst of the COVID-19 lockdown, I helped set up a GoFundMe to help Dan and my sister-in-law Sue with their upcoming medical bills. When Sue asked me if I could sit with Dan one day a week to advocate for him after his stem cell transplant, it provided me with "something" that I could do. I said yes. I tried to focus on the positive: because of all the safety protocols to get into his room, it was a great excuse to buy a new pair of Crocs flats. They were stylish AND could be disinfected with Lysol!

On my first shift with Dan, I told him that I had found the perfect fight song for him: "Don't Stop" by Fleetwood Mac.

The lyrics demanded that he set his sights on tomorrow. It offered a message of hope.

During my hospital shifts, I told him stories and jokes, quizzed him on trivia, and sometimes bored him to sleep. While he slept, I worked on sewing projects or read a book. I nagged him to drink water and to walk the halls. I made him homemade apple crisp, because he said the hospital's version was awful. I even brought him some "full moon water" to help with his recovery. I watched him hide his fear and pain from me, always trying to maintain that "big brother has it all under control" image. When he did break down on occasion, it broke my heart. It was my job to shore him up. My goal was to make him laugh.

My experience as a caregiver during my brother's stem cell transplant recovery was painfully hard, and awkward, and eye-opening, and terrifying. This was new territory to conquer. But I held on to the belief that my brother was perfect, and that he was going to beat cancer. I kept telling myself, "Don't stop thinking about tomorrow." I am grateful that he still has lots of tomorrows to remind me of how perfect he is.

His Son- Nicholas

If I could title my portion and experience over the last 5+ years, I would quote a line from one of my favorite bands (Yellowcard) "try to breathe the air that's here and now." I believe that's a perfect line because that's the attitude I tried to have every day with my father. Soak up every moment, good or bad, because this is the time we have together.

When my father was first diagnosed with myelofibrosis, there were only unknowns to me. My parents either kept certain information away from us or weren't good at communicating exactly what was going on. It was the early moments of our experience, so I didn't fault them, and secretly I didn't want to know the details then, anyway. In addition, demanding details and asking too many questions can add stress and anxiety to the patient and caregiver (dad and mom in my case), so I tried to give it time. I knew cancer is a killer, and my thoughts primarily started with, "I may not have my father for long."

No matter how this was going to turn out, my brothers and I were determined to give my father some great memories and ramp up our time with him. Despite not being a racing fan, I was happy to drive out to Indianapolis for the Indy 500. My father and I stopped in Canton, Ohio, on the way to see the Pro Football Hall of Fame. I had a wonderful time with my father on that trip, and we lived in the moment as best we could. Despite the ramp-up of attention, it was also essential to keep a normalcy level for my parents. We pretended life was business as usual as best we could.

I remember meeting up with a friend before my father started his procedure. Unfortunately, her father had gone through cancer treatments and would pass away. She gave me all sorts of advice, but the one that stuck with me was that as a secondary caregiver, my job should focus more on taking care of the primary caregiver than the patient. I made it my primary goal to be there for my mother, distract her when I could, and give her breaks. My mother took her role very seriously, so getting her not to feel guilty about taking breaks was difficult, but the respite was needed. Driving to Philadelphia to be with my father on Fridays gave my mother a day to look forward to in some sense so she could rest. I also wanted to see him, anyway. Making sure the lights were on, and the door was unlocked when she came home just gave her one less thing to think about. Cleaning every day, organizing medications, shopping, and making food were all tasks that could be shared. It allowed her to come home and sit in a quiet room or be able to turn on the tv and rest.

In addition to doing my best for my mother and keeping the primary caregiver going strong, it was also essential to make sure my father knew everything was taken care of at home. As a father and homeowner, he had concerns when it came to house care and car care. Pictures and stories of how things were getting done at home while he was in the hospital would hopefully give him some mental rest as well. Anything I thought I could do to allow my parents some mental rest became important to me.

When my father came home, not much changed for me. I was happy to have him home, but I was also scared that he was now in our hands, not professionally trained people. Each day consisted of doing my best to care for my mother and learning my father's care processes. We set up an alert system where if my father needed anything, he could click a button, and bells would sound across the house. The bell system put me at ease a little bit, so I didn't need to check on him constantly. As we look forward, I will try to keep the same mantra, "try to breathe the air that's here and now."

'. Enjoy each day I have with my family and take the lessons I learned from my father's cancer and trials.

His Son- Eric

I was at work when I found out about Dad's cancer. I was changing a water meter in Pottsville, PA. When I got a text from my mom with the news, it hit me hard because I had been convinced that his problems had other explanations. I cried a little and then prayed. Later that day, I researched what his condition meant for him in the long term. It looked awful, and one of the biggest things that stuck out to me was that the condition had no cure, and the average life expectancy after prognosis was only a couple of years. I cried and prayed again in my work truck, and the thoughts about losing my dad were overwhelming.

I thought about what this meant for my family, especially for mom. If I was overwhelmed, what did she feel? That's when I first became a caregiver. I knew my role would be to help them through the complex parts of this journey and be a level-headed and objective voice.

Aside from conversations and family meetings, I didn't have much of a role until Dad went into the hospital. On admissions day, I drove my parents to Penn and waited with them in Radiology. Mom had stepped away for a minute when Dad was called back to have his PICC line placed. Neither of them liked needles, so they were both thankful I offered to go back with him. They had both thought the PICC line was a simple needle in a vein like you would get for a regular hospital visit: they were wrong! My dad wasn't going back to get a small needle inserted into a vein; he was being prepped for surgery where they were running a 12-18" line from his arm directly into his heart! I'm not going to lie; with my sense of humor (which I got from my dad), I laughed out loud. We were not expecting this, and my dad and I have always connected through our humor. I had taken a picture of him in that waiting room before the nurse came in to tell him "The news." And after!

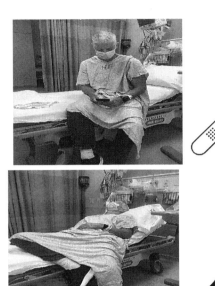

I would use humor a lot to help my parents through the more difficult times. It was a way to connect with my dad and take some of the pressure off myself.

Having a family of my own and working full time didn't allow me a lot of time to help with the day-to-day things. While dad was in the hospital, I would visit once a week for the day. We would just sit in the room together and watch tv. While he napped, I would work on my computer or nap myself. Occasionally, I had to force my dad to go for a walk around the unit to stretch his legs.

When I wasn't at the hospital, I helped my mom with house projects and had the kids around to keep her entertained. My brothers took care of the general maintenance of the home. All seemed to fall into a rhythm together as dad moved through the process.

After Hurricane Ida in the fall of 2021, I was relocated for work in Louisiana. My parents came to visit in the Spring of 2022 to help with our relief work. Dad helped drive the fork-lift to place roofing shingles on a flatbed trailer and went out to the Jobsite.

That was the day I realized my dad's caregiver days, for me, were finished. My dad was back to helping me! It was a joyous and somber moment. I spent some time reflecting on his journey, and is still on, we were back to a normal father and son who had other things to do besides worry about cancer!

Dan

To start with, I'll state the obvious; I am alive! My perspective on this will, in all probability, be odd to you. Few times since my diagnosis have I thought that this struggle was about me. When I was informed that I had some kind of blood cancer, my first thoughts were," I'm going to die, that's okay, I'm in my late 50s, my kids are grown, I'm ready." Nobody in my circle felt the same way. I heard many times, "You're young, you're strong, you can beat this!"

Multiple people worked harder to keep me alive than I did. It's easier to struggle than to watch a loved one struggle. Through many frustrations, setbacks, and heartbreaks, I fought my way through not letting down those supporting me. Of course, self-preservation is a natural state of being, so the internal turmoil haunted me.

As a caregiver, patience will be your most valuable asset. The same might be true for someone dealing with blood cancer. I understood that I would be sicker given chemotherapy and radiation. I understood I would be in recovery for up to a year. The reality would be quite different.

As a patient, do whatever's required of you. Love and care

for those that love and care for you. Recovery or not, these personality attributes will serve you.

In Remembrance

*"Many people will walk in and out of your life,
but only true friends will leave footprints in the heart."*
Eleanor Roosevelt

William Pascal Brown 2020
Dad to Sue

Annmarie (Maiorino) Williams 2020
Friend

Michelle Ballenger Ryan (Mimi)
(Erin's mom) 2018

Almira Mae (Yates) 2018
Cousin to Sue

Everett Richard Dick Yates 2018
Uncle to Sue

Almira Foster Richer 2019
Aunt to Sue

DONATION

Contributions may be made in Michelle's memory to
Samaritan Hospice, 5 Eves Dr, Suite 300, Marlton, NJ 08053

(If you would like to donate to Michelle's 5 grandchildren
contact Erinryan12@yahoo.com)
The Williams Family Fund
Medford Lakes NJ 08055
Web: http://PayPal.me/williamsfamilyfund

All Book Proceeds go to Dan's continued care
and Cancer Research

Thank you

Made in United States
Orlando, FL
29 August 2022

21706336R00115

CHAPTER 8

STARTED A LOGBOOK for the caregivers. We could write what we thought was important to share for the next caregiver shift. Often, I came in and saw something that helped me understand what had happened during the last few days. We also began a caregiver group text, which kept us all in the loop. Both helped, especially on days Dan was not capable of sharing. His memory was in and out. Nurses struggled with keeping his blood pressure stable and other vital signs. It was beneficial to know this information since we often had to share it with the nurses that came in. (Information was on the in-room computer, but not all nurses were assigned to Dan.) The logbook also helped when speaking with a Team member when visiting. I had to refer to it several times to share information they did not have. Although the nurses were excellent, some missed significant concerns or at least concerns I thought were important.

Logbook Entries (Copied directly from the notebook):
Thursday, September 24th, 2020, Caregiver
Dayna (sister)

Logbook - "In at 9:30 am Dan hooked up w/magnesium & took a bunch of pills (anti-nausea, antibiotics ~c.) He ordered his lunch and dinner for today and brea¹ tomorrow. He is expecting a shot to lower his white is in great spirits today 😊 His White blood count is 10.1 (down from 35.0 on 9/18) After lunch walked 3 laps & showered. Slept from 1:00pm to 3:00pm. 3:30 2 more laps while linen was changed. Social Worker came in for an interview at @3:45. His blood pressure is a little elevated."

Friday, September 25th, 2020, Caregiver Tim (son)

Birthday Day or 0. Had radiation at 8:00 am this morning. Brushed teeth after breakfast. Blood pressure down from yesterday 129/78. He ate ½ of his salmon lunch at noon, brushed his teeth, and used saltwater rinse at 12:50 pm. Stem cells were injected at 1:20om. Done with stem cells at 1:53 pm." **Here we go!**

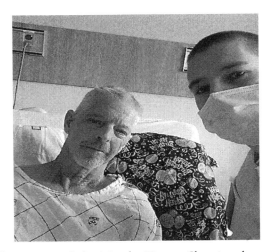

Pillowcase made by Marsha Krone. She gives hope on the Facebook MPN group! Has made and given hundreds.